Preface

The Welfare Food Scheme was introduced in 1940 as a wartime measure to help ensure the provision of an adequate diet under rationing conditions. Today, the Scheme provides milk and vitamins in kind, primarily to expectant and nursing mothers and children aged under 5 in 'low income families'. Over a fifth of the nation's children aged under 5 qualify for the scheme, a fact that must raise a number of important and wide-ranging questions.

In 1999, the Government decided to review the Welfare Foods Scheme – the first and only major review in the Scheme's 60-year history. It was particularly timely in light of accumulating evidence on the influence of early nutrition on risk of developing non-insulin dependent diabetes, hypertension and coronary heart disease. The *Independent Inquiry into Inequalities in Health* also outlined how inequalities in nutrition in women and children influence health and recommended that a high priority be given to policies aimed at improving the health and nutrition of women of childbearing age and their children.

The Committee on Medical Aspects of Food and Nutrition Policy's (COMA) Panel on Child and Maternal Nutrition was asked to undertake a scientific review of the Scheme particularly the nutritional aspects. The report, which was completed in 2000, concluded that the scheme retains great potential for improving the health of the pregnant women, nursing mothers and young children from disadvantaged groups in the population. The panel recommended some important changes to the Scheme in order to address the present-day nutritional vulnerabilities of these groups.

I welcome this report and am most grateful to Dr Anthony Williams, who chaired the Group. I commend the members of the Panel for undertaking this task within a short time scale and generously giving their time and expertise to this very comprehensive report.

PROFESSOR SIR JOHN GRIMLEY EVANS
Chairman, Committee on Medical Aspects of Food and Nutrition Policy

iv

Department of Health

Report on Health and Social Subjects

51

Scientific Review of the Welfare Food Scheme

Report of the Committee on Medical Aspects of Food and Nutrition Policy
Report of the Panel on Child and Maternal Nutrition of the Committee on
Medical Aspects of Food and Nutrition Policy

London : TSO

Published by TSO (The Stationery Office) and available from:

Online
www.tso.co.uk/bookshop

Mail, Telephone, Fax & E-mail
TSO
PO Box 29, Norwich, NR3 1GN
Telephone orders/General enquiries: 0870 600 5522
Fax orders: 0870 600 5533
E-mail: book.orders@tso.co.uk
Textphone 0870 240 3701

TSO Shops
123 Kingsway, London, WC2B 6PQ
020 7242 6393 Fax 020 7242 6394
68-69 Bull Street, Birmingham B4 6AD
0121 236 9696 Fax 0121 236 9699
9-21 Princess Street, Manchester M60 8AS
0161 834 7201 Fax 0161 833 0634
16 Arthur Street, Belfast BT1 4GD
028 9023 8451 Fax 028 9023 5401
18-19 High Street, Cardiff CF10 1PT
029 2039 5548 Fax 029 2038 4347
71 Lothian Road, Edinburgh EH3 9AZ
0870 606 5566 Fax 0870 606 5588

TSO Accredited Agents
(see Yellow Pages)

and through good booksellers

Published with the permission of the Department of Health on behalf of the Controller of Her Majesty's Stationery Office.

First published 2002

ISBN 0 11 322589 X

Printed in the United Kingdom for The Stationery Office
107340, C15, 09/02

Contents

Committee on Medical Aspects of Food and Nutrition Policy

Chair

Professor Sir John Grimley Evans   Division of Clinical Geratology, Nuffield Department of Clinical Medicine, University of Oxford

Members

Professor P Aggett   Head of Lancashire Postgraduate School of Medicine and Health, University of Central Lancashire

Professor S Bingham   Deputy Director, MRC Dunn Human Nutrition Unit, Cambridge

Professor G Fowler   Professor Emeritus of General Practice, University of Oxford

Professor A A Jackson   Professor of Human Nutrition, University of Southampton

Professor W P T James   Director, Rowett Research Institute, Aberdeen (until June 1999)

Professor M Marmot   Professor of Epidemiology and Public Health, University College Medical School, London

Professor D P Richardson   Nestle UK Limited, Croydon, Surrey

Dr P Troop   Regional Director of Public Health, Anglia and Oxford, Milton Keynes (until September 1999)

Dr A F Williams   Senior Lecturer and Consultant in Neonatal Paediatrics, St George's Hospital, London

Assessors

Professor L Donaldson	Chief Medical Officer for England
Dr H Campbell	Chief Medical Officer, DHSS Northern Ireland
Professor Sir David Carter	Chief Medical Officer, Department of Health, Scottish Office
Dr R Hall	Chief Medical Officer, Department of Health, Welsh Office
Dr A Peatfield	Medical Research Council
Mr G Podger	Ministry of Agriculture, Fisheries and Food
Dr E Rubery	Department of Health (until July 1999)
Ms K Peploe	Health Education Authority (from October 1999)

Secretariat from the Department of Health

Dr S Reddy (Scientific)

Mr B Wenlock (Scientific)

Miss Yemi Fagun (Administrative)

Miss C Dick (Scientific)

Miss S Kunar (Scientific)

Miss S Collaco (Administrative)

Committee on Medical Aspects of Food and Nutrition Policy:

Panel on Child and Maternal Nutrition

Chairman

Dr Anthony Williams — St George's Hospital, London

Members

Dr Anne Aukett — Northern Birmingham Community NHS Trust

Dr Clare Goodhart — Statham Grove Surgery, London

Professor Peter Howie — Ninewells Hospital and Medical School, Dundee

Ms Pat Margiotta — University of Salford, Manchester

Ms Vanessa Shaw — Great Ormond Street Hospital for Children, London

Professor Mary Renfrew — University of Leeds, Leeds

Professor M Stuart Tanner — University of Sheffield, Sheffield

Dr Valerie Walker — Southampton General Hospital, Southampton

Professor Lawrence Weaver — Royal Hospital for Sick Children, Glasgow

Observers

Dr Ian Bashford — Scottish Executive

Dr Margaret Boyle — DHSS Northern Ireland

Mrs Kathleen Dawson — Department of Health

Dr Jane Ludlow	Welsh Assembly
Dr Sue Martin	Department of Health
Ms Catherine McCormick	Department of Health
Dr Alison Redfern	MAFF

Secretariat

Ms Anna Taylor	Consultant, Department of Health
Mr Robert Wenlock	Department of Health
Dr Sheela Reddy	Department of Health
Miss Sarbjit Kunar	Department of Health
Mrs Carole Walker	Administrative

Acknowledgements

The Panel is grateful to the following who provided contributions on request:

Phyll Buchanan	The Breastfeeding Network
Professor Tim Cole	Institute of Child Health, London
Rosemary Burbridge	National Childbirth Trust
Gillian Dollamore	Office of National Statistics, London
Dr Elizabeth Dowler	London School of Hygiene and Tropical Medicine
Nigel Fisek	Office of National Statistics, London
Fiona Ford	University of Sheffield, Sheffield
Andrew Fox	Department for Education and Employment, London
Kevin Hawthorne	Department of Social Security, London
Dr Fiona Mathews	Oxford University, Oxford
Dr Ann Prentice	MRC Human Nutrition Research, Cambridge
Dr Charlotte Wright	University of Newcastle-upon-Tyne

Glossary

ALSPAC   Avon Longitudinal Study on Pregnancy and Childhood

BMI   Body mass index, (weight /height^2)

Breastmilk substitute   Any food being marketed or otherwise represented as a partial or total replacement for breastmilk, whether or not suitable for that purpose (WHO, 1981)

COMA   The Committee on Medical Aspects of Food and Nutrition Policy

Complementary foods   Foods other than breastmilk or infant formula

DH   Department of Health

DRV   Dietary Reference Value, a generic term which covers LRNI, EAR, RNI and safe intake (see below)

DSS   Department of Social Security

EAR   Estimated Average Requirement of a group of people for any nutrient. About half will usually need more than the EAR and half less

Exclusive breastfeeding   The infant receives only breastmilk and no other liquids or solids with the exception of vitamin or mineral supplements, or medicines (WHO, 1991)

FC   Family Credit. Cash benefit for families on low income with a child under 16 years, and in which at least one partner works 16 hours a week or more (Annex 2)

FTT   Failure to thrive. (This term is further defined in section 5.5.3.i)

Follow-on formula	A food intended for particular nutritional use by infants in good health aged over 4 months, and constituting the principal liquid element in a progressively diversified diet (Infant Formula and Follow-on Formula Regulations, 1995). In the United Kingdom it is recommended that follow-on formula is not used before 6 months of age (Department of Health, 1994)
GB	Great Britain, that is Wales, Scotland and England
GP	General Practitioner
HA	Health Authority
HEA	Health Education Authority
Infant	A child under the age of twelve completed months
Infant formula	A food which is intended for particular nutritional use by infants in good health during the first 4-6 months of life and satisfying by itself the nutritional requirements of such infants (Infant Formula and Follow-on Formula Regulations, 1995)
IS	Income Support. Cash benefit for people not required to be available for work, whose income is below a certain level and who work less than 16 hours a week (24 hours for partners) (Annex 2)
IBJSA	Income Based Jobseeker's Allowance. Cash benefit intended to meet the needs of unemployed people before they return to work and to help unemployed people in search of work (Annex 2)
IQ	Intelligence quotient
kcal	Kilocalories. A unit of energy 1 kcal = 4.2 kJ

LBW	Low Birth Weight. A birth weight of less than 2500 grams
Liquid milk	Whole or semi-skimmed cow's milk
Listed products	Welfare food items
LRNI	Lower Reference Nutrient Intake. The amount of a nutrient that is enough for only the few people in a group who have low needs. It is equivalent to EAR − 2(standard deviations)
MAFF	Ministry of Agriculture, Fisheries and Food
μg	micrograms
mg	milligrams
NDM	National Dried Milk
NDNS	National Diet and Nutrition Survey
NHS	National Health Service
NME	Non-milk extrinsic sugars. Extrinsic sugars are those not located within the cellular structure of a food
NSP	Non-starch polysaccharide. A precisely measurable component of foods; the best measurement of dietary fibre
NTD	Neural Tube Defect.
ONS	Office for National Statistics
PCMN	The Panel on Child and Maternal Nutrition; a standing panel of COMA
Preterm	A baby born before 37 completed weeks of gestation (259 days) from the first day of the mother's last menstrual period
RE	Retinol equivalents; 1 RE = 1 microgram retinol or 6 micrograms ß-carotene

RDA	Recommended Dietary Allowance. A term used in the the United States to indicate the nutrient intake needed to prevent deficiency in a population
RNI	Reference Nutrient Intake. The amount of a nutrient that is enough, or more than enough, for most people in a group. It is equivalent to EAR + 2(standard deviations). If the average intake of a population sub-group is at RNI, then the risk of deficiency in that group is very small
Safe intake	A term used to indicate intake or range of intakes of a nutrient for which there is not enough information to estimate EAR, RNI or LRNI. It is an amount that is enough for almost everyone but not so large as to cause undesirable effects
Social class	Social class[1] is based on occupation and employment status. Occupation is usually measured using the ONS Standard Occupational Classification and assigned a social class category: I: Professional, II: Managerial & Technical, IIIN: Skilled non-manual, IIIM: Skilled manual, IV: Partly skilled, V: Unskilled. Uncategorised groups include the armed forces, or those who inadequately describe or do not state their occupation
Solids	Non-liquid weaning or complementary foods. Some original published work has used this term. We have therefore used it in that context
The Scheme	Welfare Food Scheme
UHT	Ultra-heat treated. A term applied to liquid milk

---

[1] The new National Statistics socio-economic Classification is expected to replace the social class classification from April 2001. The Classification will be based on employment relations and conditions e.g. job security and forms of wage payment rather than on skill or concepts of manual or non-manual work

UK	United Kingdom. (Wales, Scotland, Northern Ireland and England)
Weaning	Introduction of foods other than breastmilk or infant formula
Weaning foods	Foods other than breast milk or infant formula
WIC	The United States special supplemental food programme for Women, Infants and Children
WFRU	Welfare Foods Reimbursement Unit
WFS	Welfare Food Scheme

Summary

Introduction   The COMA Panel on Maternal and Child Nutrition has undertaken the first scientific review of the Welfare Food Scheme since its inception in 1940. It has:

- reviewed current dietary recommendations,

- identified from national data, population groups vulnerable to adverse nutritional outcomes,

- evaluated the contribution of the current scheme to prevention of these vulnerabilities and

- identified further information needs and highlighted improvements likely to be cost neutral.

History and entitlement   Originally the Scheme incorporated universal provision. Subsequently it was targeted at the most socio-economically vulnerable. Today, a quarter of children under five are beneficiaries by virtue of their family's income. The Scheme has two principal beneficiary groups:

- pregnant women, mothers and young children in families eligible for certain social security benefits. With the exception of children under one year of age, all are entitled to a pint of milk a day (using redeemable milk tokens) and free vitamin supplements (available from designated clinics). Infant formula instead of milk is available for infants who are not breastfed.

- children under five years attending Scheme-registered day care facilities can receive one third of a pint of milk a day. Children aged 5-16 years not registered at school by virtue of mental or physical disability are entitled to a pint of milk a day.

Current diet and vulnerable groups   The following adverse nutritional outcomes were considered:

- *pregnant women and mothers*

  - low uptake of periconceptional folic acid supplements

  - low dietary intake during pregnancy

  - vitamin D deficiency

- *infants*

  - low levels of breastfeeding

  - early introduction of solids

  - failure to thrive

- *young children*

  - iron deficiency anaemia

  - vitamin D deficiency

  - dental caries

- *school age children*

  - poor dietary patterns

  - fatness

These outcomes were frequently associated with lower social class, low income, low maternal age, low educational attainment or ethnic minority origins.

Effect of the Scheme In addition to the nutritional contribution of welfare foods, the Scheme offers significant economic benefit to low income households. It also has potential to meet a significant proportion of nutrient intakes of all beneficiaries. The entire nutrient requirements of young infants are met by the provision of infant formula.

Uptake of vitamin supplements, potentially the most valuable Scheme product, is very low among all beneficiary groups, in contrast to milk uptake which is very high. The majority of mothers prefer to use their tokens for infant formula reflecting the low prevalence of breastfeeding. Approximately 50% of children in day care attend facilities registered with the Scheme. Children already receiving milk by virtue of their families' income may consequently receive excessive amounts of milk.

There is a need to consider the Scheme's place in the context of other public health programmes directed towards prevention of nutritional vulnerability. These include health education programmes, professional and peer support initiatives, secondary prevention (notably screening programmes), fortification of food and fluoridation of water.

Conclusions

- The Welfare Food Scheme retains great potential for improving the health of nutritionally vulnerable pregnant women, mothers and young children.

- The current provisions meet entire nutrient requirements during the first half of infancy. They therefore provide an important safety net for this group who have high growth potential and vulnerability to disease.

- Currently there is no incentive for mothers to breastfeed as the retail value of the formula allocation exceeds that of liquid milk they receive.

- Vitamin supplements are a simple, cost-effective intervention not merely for those who are current beneficiaries of the Scheme. Currently uptake is very low and improved systems of provision are needed.

- The volume of formula provided for children over 6 months exceeds requirements and could be reduced in favour of provisions which would encourage timely complementary feeding. Extension of formula provision into the second year of life would probably reduce the prevalence of iron deficiency.

- Consideration should be given to changing the formulation of vitamin preparations provided to pregnant women, breastfeeding mothers and young children.

- Provision of milk for children attending day care facilities should take account of milk entitlement at home in order to reduce the risk of excessive intake at the expense of a more varied diet.

- The individual nutritional requirements of children with special needs should be met by means more flexible than the Welfare Food Scheme.

- A package of possible modifications to the Scheme is suggested.

1. Introduction

1.1 Background

A Welfare Food Scheme has operated in the United Kingdom since 1940. It was introduced as a war-time measure to help ensure the provision of an adequate diet under rationing conditions. Originally benefits were universal, but in more recent years eligibility has been restricted to those receiving benefit, currently income based jobseekers' allowance (IBJSA), income support (IS) and family credit (FC). Currently, the Scheme provides milk and vitamins in kind, primarily to expectant and nursing mothers and children aged under 5 in 'low income families'. The number of beneficiaries in Great Britain in 1999 was approximately 55,000 pregnant women and 808,000 young children – some 23% of the estimated population sector aged 0-4 years. It cost the Exchequer in Great Britain £167 million in 1999 / 2000.

1.2 Terms of Reference

In 1999, the Government decided to review the Welfare Foods Scheme. Health Ministers agreed that the review should take the form of consultations with appropriate stakeholders supported by a number of reviews on specific aspects of the Scheme. The Committee on Medical Aspects of Food and Nutrition Policy (COMA) was asked to undertake a scientific review of the Scheme including the nutritional aspects. The COMA Panel on Child and Maternal Nutrition undertook the review.

The Terms of Reference were:

- To consider the available evidence on the current diets and nutritional status of women from conception to birth and/or the end of breastfeeding, and of children from birth to 5 years of age; and to consider whether there may be particular needs in children over the age of 5 years;

- To characterise any groups particularly vulnerable to nutritional inadequacy, and the vulnerabilities;

- To assess the contribution of Welfare Foods to maintaining adequate nutritional status;

- To identify information needs relevant to these terms of reference; and

- To report findings to the Welfare Foods Review Group, through COMA, within 4 months.

It is difficult to quantify precisely the extent to which the Scheme modifies nutritional risk. As almost all eligible families receive their entitlement there is no clear contemporaneous control group of equivalent socio-economic status. Historical comparisons are equally confounded by the huge secular changes in society over the last sixty years. While some of those nutritionally at risk today might not be beneficiaries of the current Scheme, it cannot completely address the diverse root causes of nutritional vulnerability amongst those who are. Complex and inter-related risk factors such as poverty, deprivation, low educational attainment, and language barriers are not solved by provision of food alone.

The nutritional health of pregnant women and children is important because it is increasingly accepted that early nutrition affects long-term health outcome. Sub-optimal nutrition therefore constitutes one of many mechanisms potentially perpetuating the intergenerational cycle of deprivation and disease. The recently published "*Acheson Inquiry*" recognised this and recommended "further reductions in poverty in women of child bearing age, expectant mothers, young children and older people should be made by increasing benefits in cash or in kind to them" (Acheson, 1998).

In focusing on nutritional aspects of the Scheme we fully recognise that it forms only one strand of policy aimed at improving the nutritional health of women and young children. Complementary recent initiatives have included "Cooking for kids", Regulations on National Nutritional Standards for School Lunches, foundation of breakfast clubs in "Sure Start" areas, Health Education and Health Action Zones, and an increase in the resources for breastfeeding support. In keeping with terms of reference (Chapter 1) we have reviewed the following topics to reach our conclusions:

- the history of the Scheme (Chapter 2) and its mode of operation (Chapter 3)

- successive COMA recommendations relevant to the nutritional health of children and women of childbearing age (Chapter 4)

- national data on the nutritional status, dietary practices and health of these groups [1] to gauge the extent of compliance with COMA's recommendation at a population level (Chapter 4)

- the characteristics of groups particularly "vulnerable" to nutritional inadequacy, and the underlying biological and social causes (Chapter 5)

- the contribution Welfare Foods make to the nutrient intake of beneficiaries (Chapter 6)

- other interventions operating in the UK which address nutritional vulnerability (Chapter 7)

---

[1] Where these were unavailable we have used data from local UK populations

2

This review is confined to Great Britain and does not consider the effect of the Scheme in Northern Ireland. Our conclusions about both the benefits and the shortfalls of the current scheme are summarised in Chapter 8. Recommendations for further research are made and a package of amendments to the Scheme is suggested.

2.   History

2.1   The origins of the Scheme

The Welfare Food Scheme (WFS, "the Scheme") was introduced in 1940 (DHSS, 1988) as part of the war effort. Winston Churchill said of the Scheme: "*there is no finer investment for any country than putting milk into babies*"[1]. Its wartime purpose appears to have been to safeguard the nutritional status of expectant mothers and young children (DHSS, 1988) though it also followed a four pence per gallon increase in the price of milk which provoked public "*agitation*" (Land *et al*, 1992). Much of the improvement in the well-being of children during and after the second world war was attributed to the Scheme and in 1946 the Government decided to continue it as part of the peace-time social services (Ministry of Health, 1957).

2.2   The legislative framework

The legislative basis for the Scheme was originally in the Emergency Laws. In 1986, the provision was moved to the Social Security Act and this primary legislation is supported by statutory instrument (secondary legislation) originally an *Order* and now *Regulations*. These have been frequently amended and periodically rewritten.

The most recent primary legislation (Social Security Act, 1988) defines "welfare foods" as meaning "*liquid cow's milk, infant formula, vitamin tablets and vitamin drops. It provides that the Secretary of State may by order add to or remove any food...*". It also provides that "*the Secretary of State may by regulations make a scheme or a number of schemes for the provision of welfare food and for the making of payments to such persons as may be determined by or under the scheme who are entitled to receive a welfare food but who:*

(i)   *do not receive it*

(ii)   *do not receive the amount to which they are so entitled*"

The secondary legislation was consolidated within the Welfare Food Regulations in 1996 in Great Britain and details of their provisions are noted in Chapter 3. The legislation covers Great Britain but some administrative functions are devolved to Scotland and Wales. Northern Ireland has its own legislation for Welfare Foods which is broadly in line with provisions in Great Britain (Welfare Food Regulations (Northern Ireland), 1988).

---

[1] Quote from Churchill in original footage shown on "*Newsnight*" 23/9/98

2.3   Changes made to the Scheme since 1940

The recent legislation documents the modifications made to the Scheme from 1940 to the present day. Since its inception key changes have occurred in the nature of the welfare foods themselves and in the defined beneficiary population.

2.3.1   Changes in welfare foods

Foods initially included were: liquid milk, national dried milk (NDM), concentrated orange juice and cod liver oil. These were provided free or at reduced cost depending on the recipient. In the 1940s dried eggs were added for children under 5 years. NDM was manufactured under licence from the government and used for feeding infants. It was not until the 1970s that the forerunners of today's infant formula were presented as an alternative to NDM (DHSS, 1974; WFS, 1995). In 1977, National Dried Milk was withdrawn and a list of suitable infant formulas, based on advice from COMA, was publicised. Arrangements were made for infants who had qualified for NDM free of charge to have the newer modified low solute foods also free of charge for the first year of life (DHSS, 1980). Any additions of infant formulas to the list are normally based on advice from COMA's Panel on Child and Maternal Nutrition (PCMN).

Cod liver oil was removed from the list of welfare foods when the 1971 Welfare Food Order was rewritten in 1975. Vitamin drops and tablets containing vitamins A and D had been inserted in previous Orders as an alternative to cod liver oil and became a substitute for cod liver oil in the 1975 Order. Orange juice was also omitted from the 1975 Order and vitamin C was added as a third component of the vitamin drops and tablets.

2.3.2   Changes in beneficiaries

The Welfare Food Scheme began as a *universal* programme for all children under five years, pregnant and lactating women, regardless of family income. The additional provisions for nursery school and disabled children date back at least to the 1950s. Some were eligible for free welfare foods and the remainder for subsidised foods. The criteria for entitlement have changed over time. In 1968, beneficiaries entitled to free welfare foods were called *"families in special circumstances"* and described as those for whom *"requirements exceeded resources"* (Welfare Foods Order, 1968). In 1971 when Social Security legislation was passed new categories of beneficiaries developed to include those on Supplementary Benefit (SB) and Family Income Supplements (FIS). There was a discretionary inclusion of Low Income Families. Free and subsidised provisions for each group varied over time but welfare foods were free for all those on SB and FIS by the 1980s.

The 1988 Social Security Act made changes to welfare provision and the Scheme. Provisions for those receiving SB (which became "Income Support", IS) did not change but those on FIS now received Family Credit (FC). Their entitlement to welfare foods changed to a monetary allowance incorporated into Family Credit, set at the cost of liquid milk and school dinners for children aged 0-16 years. As a result of this change those receiving FC who wish to use infant formula in the first year of life have to pay back the equivalent of the liquid milk value from their FC allowance in order to receive free infant formula (Department of Health, 1998a).

2.4   **Reviews of the Scheme**

The Scheme has been scrutinised previously, usually on the basis that it is out of date and costly. Although further revisions have been proposed since restricting the beneficiary criteria they have never been implemented. The only scientific consideration was the Joint Committee on Welfare Foods review of the non-milk components of the Scheme in 1957. It recommended that vitamins A,C and D continue to be components of the Scheme (Ministry of Health, 1957).

2.5   **Summary**

The Welfare Food Scheme has been in place since 1940 but the nature of the foods provided has been only slightly modified. Vitamin drops have been substituted for cod liver oil and orange juice, and infant formula has replaced "national dried" milk. The major change of beneficiary group involved the shift from a universal programme to one targeted at the economically vulnerable, as defined by social security provisions. In this review we examine whether this economic criterion adequately defines nutritional risk among young women and children in the population of the United Kingdom.

3. Description of the current scheme

3.1 Entitlement

3.1.1 Families in receipt of Income Support or Income Based Jobseeker's Allowance [1], expectant mothers and children under 5 years in families receiving income support (IS) or income-based jobseeker's allowance (IBJSA) may receive the following, free of charge:

- *Milk.* Beneficiaries receive a milk token per week, which may be exchanged for 7 pints (4 litres) of liquid milk [2]. Infants under one year who are being bottle-fed may receive instead 900 grams per week of an infant formula chosen from nine listed brands [3]. There is no way of ensuring that liquid cow's milk is not given to a baby under one year of age.

- *Vitamin supplements.* Expectant mothers, breastfeeding mothers (up to a year post partum) and children under 5 are entitled to free vitamins. The composition of tablets and drops differs, particularly in relation to vitamin A content (Table 3.1). Drops are recommended for pregnant women and children under five years; tablets for breastfeeding women.

Infant formula and vitamin supplements provided under the scheme are available only from health authority/NHS community trust clinics and welfare food

Table 3.1: Nutrient content of vitamin supplements

	Nutrient content of 1 ml [4] of vitamin drop	Daily dose of vitamin drops (5 drops) for pregnant women, children under five years and breastfeeding mothers.	Nutrient content of 1 vitamin tablet (daily dose) for breastfeeding mothers
Vitamin A (RE)	1500µg	214µg	1200µg
Vitamin D	50 µg	7.15µg	10µg
Vitamin C	150mg	21.4mg	60mg
Calcium	-	-	40mg
Iodine	-	-	0.13mg potassium iodide

---

[1] The basis for entitlement to Income Support and Income Based Job Seeker's Allowance is shown in Annex 2

[2] Liquid milk means whole or semi-skimmed liquid cow's milk including long-life or UHT milk but not fully skimmed milk. Liquid milk is available under the Welfare Food Scheme from a wide range of shops and milk roundsmen in exchange for tokens (section 3.2.2)

[3] The brands and nutrient content of the formulas are listed in Annex 1. Follow-on, soy based or formulas for premature babies are not currently available on the Scheme

[4] 1 ml of vitamin supplement is approximately 35 drops

distribution centres designated by the local health authority/health board or NHS Trust. Vitamin supplements are listed in the British National Formulary and can also be prescribed. If purchased at a clinic they cost approximately 60 pence (for 10ml or 45 tablets).

3.1.2   Families in receipt of Family Credit [1]
Parents of children aged under 1 year are entitled to purchase from clinics 900 grams of infant formula per week at a reduced price (£3.90 from October 1999).

3.1.3   Children Under 5 years old in Daycare Facilities
The Welfare Food Scheme also enables children under 5 years old to receive free of charge 200 ml (one third of a pint) of liquid milk each day they attend daycare facilities for two hours or more. Babies under 1 year may receive the same amount of infant formula. These amounts are additional to any provided under the terms of section 3.1.1.

3.1.4   Disabled Children
Parents of a child aged 5 to 16 years who *"because of physical or mental disability is not a registered pupil at a school"* may claim milk tokens exchangeable for 4 litres (7 pints) of liquid milk per week. This component of the Scheme may have been overlooked when the provision of free school milk was withdrawn in the 1970s. Currently only 36 children are registered nationally.

3.1.5   Special groups

3.1.5.i   *Mothers under 18 years*
Pregnant women and mothers under 18 years have the following entitlement to benefits:

- Women under the age of 16 years are not entitled to any social security benefits [2] in their own right if they become pregnant. However, if their parents are receiving IS or IBJSA, they can claim welfare foods for a pregnant teenager.

- Unemployed 16 and 17 year olds are not usually entitled to benefits as they have an allocated Youth Training Place. However they are entitled to receive IBJSA if forced to live away from home and certain severe hardship conditions are satisfied.

- A pregnant woman aged 16 or 17 years is entitled to IS within 11 weeks of her expected confinement as she is not required to be available for work.

---

[1] The basis for entitlement to Family Credit is shown in Annex 2

[2] These women are entitled to support from Local Authorities if their children are classified as *children in need* under the 1989 Children Act

- A mother aged 16-17 years is entitled to IS if a lone parent or IBJSA if she has a qualifying partner and a child.

To summarise: No pregnant woman or mother under the age of 16 years can receive welfare foods unless a parent can claim for her. Pregnant women aged 16-17 years can only receive them within 11 weeks of the expected date of confinement unless receiving IBJSA. All mothers over 16 years who have children under five years are entitled to welfare foods as long as they meet the income criteria for IS or IBJSA (Annex 2).

3.1.5.ii *Refugees*
The 1996 Asylum and Immigration Act removed access to IS (and therefore Welfare Foods):

- for those who did not declare an asylum application until after they had entered the country

- to port applicants at the point at which their asylum application was refused.

Those not eligible for IS are dependent on local authority social services departments under the terms of the National Assistance Act 1948, the Children Act 1989, the Social Work Act (Scotland) 1968 and the Children Act (Scotland) 1995. In April 2000, 8,800 families of asylum seekers will probably not be eligible for IS (Home Office, 1999).

It is anticipated that an Immigration and Asylum Bill will be enacted in 2000. A new Directorate will then be responsible for support of all asylum seekers. All will be entitled on the basis of need to subsistence based on 70% of the value of IS. Support will be in the form of vouchers with a small cash component (£7 per week for adults, £3.50 for children over 3 years and £7.00 for children under 3 years). Special arrangements for applicants with special needs (such as pregnant women) may be incorporated (Home Office, 1999). Asylum seekers as a group will not be beneficiaries of the Scheme. In contrast, those who have been granted leave to remain or given refugee status are entitled to IS and therefore have access to the Scheme.

3.2   Administration

3.2.1   Distribution of Milk Tokens
Milk tokens are issued to eligible families in receipt of IS or IBJSA. On receipt of a new application the Benefits Agency (BA) assesses eligibility and calculates the cash amount awarded to reflect the number of children aged under 5 years. Proportionate entitlement to Welfare Foods is then automatically awarded and BA marks each order book or Giro cheque with the appropriate number of milk tokens. The beneficiary usually receives tokens when cashing his/her IS or IBJSA Giro cheque/order at the local Post Office (under a DH contract with Post Office Counters Ltd). Each token bears two boxes: one depicting a bottle of liquid milk, the other a tin of dried baby milk. The beneficiary states which type of milk

he/she requires. Post Office counter staff then validate each token by date-stamping the appropriate box. It remains valid for 4 weeks. If IS/IBJSA customers opt instead to have benefit paid directly into a bank account by automated credit transfer, local BA offices date stamp and issue milk tokens to WFS beneficiaries by post.

3.2.2   Distribution of Liquid Milk

A token validated for liquid milk can be exchanged with any retail supplier (any organisation or person who sells milk to the general public) willing to accept it. In 1929 there were around 20,000 liquid milk retailers participating in the Scheme. Each token can be exchanged for 7 pints (or 4 litres) of cow's milk (see section 3.1.1).

In order to claim reimbursement the retailer sends the tokens with a completed claim form to the Welfare Foods Reimbursement Unit (WFRU) which is operated by a private company under contract to the GB Health Departments. WFRU counts the tokens and pays the suppliers. In Northern Ireland, the milk suppliers are reimbursed by United Dairy Farmers.

3.2.3   Purchase and Distribution of Infant Formula and Vitamins

In most areas of Great Britain, beneficiaries obtain infant formula and vitamins from maternity and child health clinics. They may be asked to demonstrate entitlement by producing documentary evidence such as an order book or award letter from BA and proof of their child's age. Health Authorities (Health Boards in Scotland) provide for the supply of infant formula in their areas in accordance with section 3(1)(d) of the National Health Service Act 1977 and Regulations 2 and 3 of and Schedule 1 to the National Health Service (Functions of Health Authorities and Administration Arrangements) Regulation 1996 together with health service guidelines HSG(95)30. Health Authorities/Health Boards and NHS trusts may also make local distribution arrangements through non-clinic outlets. Local community pharmacies have been the choice in some areas; other examples are local retailers and GPs' premises. This arrangement allows some flexibility to take account of local need.

The NHS Supplies Authority (NHS SA), acting on behalf of the Health Departments, negotiates prices with the manufacturers of infant formula and has a strong bargaining position as WFS accounts for around 30 per cent of United Kingdom total dried baby milk sales. Vitamins similarly are bought directly by the NHS SA from specialist manufacturers and do not bear marketing costs or retail profit. Health Authorities/Health Boards and Community Trusts in England submit a quarterly claim form (WF6) to the Department of Health to be reimbursed for infant formula and vitamins supplied to WFS beneficiaries. In England the Department of Health checks these claim forms; Scottish Executive Health Department and Welsh Assembly do likewise in their respective domains. In Northern Ireland, Trusts submit claims on a quarterly basis and are reimbursed by the Health Service Executive.

3.2.4   Distribution of Nursery Milk

Daycare providers are not required to take part in the Scheme and those wishing to take part must first apply to WFRU for approval. By no means all do so. Once approved they submit claim forms every 4 months to be reimbursed the cost of milk supplied. These are checked and paid by WFRU or the Health Service Executive in Northern Ireland. There is no specific provision for children in care or foster care.

3.2.5   Distribution of milk for disabled children

The Disability Benefits Unit DBU administers this part of the Scheme on behalf of the Health Departments in Great Britain. In Northern Ireland the Health Service Executive carries out this function. Currently only 36 children in the UK are involved.

The parent/guardian must complete an application form and return it together with a copy of the child's birth certificate. DBU checks the form and confirms with the local education authority that the child is unable by virtue of disability to attend school. On verification DBU issue a 12 month stock of tokens validated for successive weeks. After this period beneficiaries must reapply.

3.3   **Costs of the scheme**

Table 2 indicates the costs of the Scheme in 1997/8 in Great Britain. The cost of formula milk for IS and IBJSA beneficiaries far exceeds that for families on FC. Expenditure on vitamins constitutes less than 0.02% of the total budget. Administration amounts to almost 10% of overall costs.

Table 3.2 : Costs of the WFS in Great Britain

EXPENDITURE 1997/98		£ MILLION
WELFARE FOODS		
Liquid cow's milk	Income support / IBJSA	100.325
	Nursery milk	12.296
	Disabled children	0.005
Formula milk	Income Support / IBJSA	37.333
	Family Credit	3.907
Vitamins		0.032
TOTAL WELFARE FOODS		**153.898**
ADMINISTRATION		
Post Office Counters Ltd		4.774
Welfare Foods Reimbursement Unit (WFRU)		0.916
Postage		0.136
NHS Supplies Authority		0.040
The Benefits Agency*		0.538
The Stationery Office		0.508
NHS (built into revenue allocations)**		6.343
Department of Health, Scottish Executive and Welsh Assembly staff costs (including fraud prevention)		0.218
TOTAL ADMIN		**13.473**
GRAND TOTAL		**167.371**

* The total cost of this service for 1997/8 was £0.706 million. Benefits met the remaining £0.168 million

** 1995/6 figures based on survey of Health Authorities and uprated to 1997/8 values

3.4   Conclusions

- Recipients of IS and IBJSA have different welfare food entitlements to welfare foods than those on FC (sections 3.1.1 and 3.1.2).

- As younger pregnant women have higher nutritional requirements (section 4.4.1) it seems illogical that those under 16 years of age have no entitlement to the Scheme, and that those aged 17-18 years have reduced entitlement (section 3.1.5.i).

- The Scheme accounts for approximately one-third of the infant formula market in the United Kingdom and almost a quarter of children under one year are entitled to this milk (Chapter 1).

- The system for distributing vitamins and infant formula poses administrative problems because much child surveillance now occurs outside recognised distribution centres. It has been suggested that this might explain low uptake of vitamin supplements (sections 3.2.3 and 6.2.1.ii).

- The allowance for children in daycare facilities is additional to any already received by families receiving IS and IBJSA (sections 3.1.3 and 6.4.1.iii). This could result in children consuming large quantities of cow's milk at the expense of a more varied diet.

- Refugee children, potentially a nutritionally vulnerable group, are entitled to welfare foods only if their family is eligible for IS. The many refugee families not eligible for this benefit have no entitlement to Welfare Foods (section 3.1.5.ii).

- Very few children nationally receive the allowance for disability (sections 3.1.4).

- Administration accounts for almost 10% of the Scheme costs, whereas the cost of vitamins, potentially the most valuable nutritional component, is insignificant (section 3.3).

4. Dietary recommendations and current practice

4.1 Terms of reference

"To consider the available evidence on the current diets and nutritional status of women from conception to birth and/or the end of breastfeeding, and of children from birth to 5 years of age; and to consider whether there may be particular needs in children over the age of 5 years"

4.2 Background

This chapter summarises current dietary recommendations for women between conception and the end of breastfeeding, and those for children up to 18 years of age. They are then set against available national data on dietary practices and nutrient intakes.

4.2.1 Sources and history of recommendations

Dietary Reference Values for Food Energy and Nutrients for the United Kingdom (Department of Health, 1991) defines levels of nutrient intake consistent with the prevention of deficiency in the UK population. The 1991 report has been supplemented by four further publications: *Folic Acid and the Prevention of Neural Tube Defects* (Department of Health, 1992), *Weaning and the Weaning Diet* (Department of Health, 1994), *Nutrition and Bone Health* (Department of Health, 1998) and *Folic Acid and the prevention of disease* (Department of Health, 2000). The other reports considered aspects of dietary patterns and lifestyle and made recommendations additional to those of the 1991 report.

4.2.2 Sources of evidence on current diet

The following national data on current dietary practice are relevant to the groups considered in this report:

- The quinquennial Infant Feeding Surveys (last conducted in 1995 (Foster *et al*, 1997)).

- The Infant feeding in Asian families Survey conducted 1994-5 (Thomas & Avery, 1997).

- The National Diet and Nutrition Survey (NDNS): children aged 1½–4½ years conducted 1992-3 (Gregory *et al*, 1995).

- The National Diet and Nutrition Survey (NDNS): young people aged 4-18 years (conducted 1997/8) – Great Britain. The Panel had limited access to preliminary data from this survey as the findings had not been published.

- The Food and Nutrient Intakes of British Infants aged 6-12 months (conducted 1986) – Great Britain (Mills & Tyler, 1992).

- The National Dietary and Nutritional Survey of British adults (conducted 1986-7) – Great Britain (Gregory et al, 1990; MAFF, 1994).

- Health Survey for England 1995-7: The Health of Young People (Prescott-Clark & Primatesta, 1998).

There are no national data on the dietary intakes of pregnant women or lactating women. The Survey of British Adults specifically excluded pregnant women and only ten lactating women were included.

4.3   Conception

4.3.1   Recommendations
Incremental DRVs developed for pregnancy *"depend at least in part on the adequacy of the pre-pregnancy stores which would be expected if the pre-pregnant requirements were met"* (Department of Health, 1991). Table 4.1 and Table 4 .2 show the DRVs for nutrients for women in the reproductive age range. Where a range is given in Table 4.2 the higher figure relates to women aged 15-18 years and includes an allowance for completion of adolescent growth. The only nutrient which has a specific DRV for the time of conception is folic acid: *"all women who are planning a pregnancy should be advised to take 400µg folic acid as a daily medicinal or food supplement from when they begin trying to conceive until the twelfth week of pregnancy"* (Department of Health, 1992). For some groups, particularly those with a history of neural tube defects this is increased to 4-5mg. This is in addition to the RNI of 200µg (in Table 4.2) (Department of Health, 2000).

4.3.2   Current practice
Table 4.2 highlights the available data on dietary intakes of women in the reproductive age range and shows that for iron, potassium, magnesium and calcium at least 10% of women had intakes below the LRNI. Supplement use pre-conceptionally has not been evaluated at national level though studies of local populations are reviewed in section 5.3.1.

4.4   Pregnancy

4.4.1   Recommendations
*"DRVs reflecting any additional estimated requirement for pregnancy are given as a single incremental figure (*see Table 4.1 and Table 4.2*). For most nutrients however, no increment for pregnancy is given. This does not necessarily imply no increase in metabolic demand during pregnancy, but rather that such extra demands should be met by normal adaptation or increased efficiency of*

Table 4.1: Estimated Average Requirements for Energy: all ages

	Estimated Average Requirement (kcal per day) (Department of Health, 1991)		% whose average intake was less than Estimated Average Requirement (Gregory *et al*, 1995, Gregory *et al*, 1990 and NDNS 4-18 years in preparation)	
	Male	Female	Male	Female
0-3 months	545	515	NA	NA
4-6 months	690	645	NA	NA
7-9 months	825	765	0	0
10-12 months	920	865	0	0
1-3 years	1230	1165	67	74
4-6 years	1715	1545	78[1]	63[5]
7-10 years	1970	1740	76[2]	72[6]
11-14 years	2220	1845	76[3]	82[7]
15-18 years	2755	2110	80[4]	95[8]
19-50 years	2550	1940		71
Pregnant		+200 in last trimester		NA
Lactating: 1 month 2 months 3 months 4-6 months (Group1) 4-6 months (Group 2) >6 months (Group 1) >6 months (Group 2)		+450 +530 +570 +480 +570 +240 +550		NA

NA national data not available
See section 5.5.1 for explanation of Groups 1 & 2
[1] % <1750 kcal, [2] %< 2000kcal, [3] %<2250kcal, [4] %< 2750kcal, [5] %< 1500kcal, [6] %< 1750kcal, [7] %< 2000kcal, [8] %< 2250kcal

utilisation, or from stores of the nutrient. Indeed, in women, it is partly for such a purpose that stores are required, so removing the need for an increase in dietary intake, which in practice does not occur" (Department of Health, 1991).

DRVs which include an increment for pregnancy are energy (in the last trimester), protein, riboflavin, folate, vitamin A and vitamin D. It is assumed that increments included for thiamin and vitamin C during the last trimester will be met by increased food consumption associated with the rise in energy demands. The 10µg vitamin D increment, recently re-endorsed by COMA can only be met through supplementation (Department of Health, 1998b). In 1991 COMA specifically *"endorsed the easy availability of cheap, adequately formulated vitamin tablets for pregnant and lactating women available free to those in receipt of income support"* (Department of Health, 1991). Asian women who rarely go out and who wear fully concealing clothes have been particularly identified as having increased need for vitamin D supplements (Department of Health, 1998b).

Current recommendations indicate that alcohol consumption during pregnancy should not exceed 1-2 units once or twice a week (Department of Health, 1995).

Table 4.2: DRVs and intakes for women in the reproductive age range

	RNI 15-50 y (DH, 1991)	LRNI 15-50y (DH, 1991)	Increment for pregnancy (DH, 1991)	Increment for lactation (DH, 1991)	%<LRNI (MAFF, 1994) 16-18 y	%<LRNI (MAFF, 1994) 19-50y
Protein (g/d)	45	-	6	11, 8 **	-	-
Thiamin (mg/d)	0.8	0.45	0.1*	0.2	n.a.	n.a.
Riboflavin (mg/d)	1.1	0.8	0.3	0.5	9	8
Niacin (nicotinic acid equivalent mg/d)	13-14	8.5	-	2	n.a.	n.a.
Vitamin B6 (mg/d)	1.2	0.8***	-	-	n.a.	n.a.
Vitamin B12 (μg/d)	1.5	1.0	-	0.5	4	1
Folate (μg/d)	200•	100	100	60	4	4
Vitamin C (mg/d)	40	10	10*	30	0	1
Vitamin A (μg/d)	600	250	100	350	7	3
Vitamin D (μg/d)	-	-	10	10	-	-
Calcium (mg/d)	700-800	400-450	-	550	27	10
Phosphorus (mg/d)	550-625	300-350	-	440	n.a.	n.a.
Magnesium (mg/d)	270-300	150-190	-	50	39	13
Sodium (mg/d)	1600	575	-	-	n.a.	n.a.
Potassium (mg/d)	3500	2000	-	-	30	27
Chloride (mg/d)	2500	890	-	-	n.a.	n.a.
Iron (mg/d)	14.8	8.0	-	-	33	26
Zinc (mg/d)	7.0	4.0	-	6.0, 2.5**	6	4
Copper (mg/d)	1.0-1.2	-	-	0.3	-	-
Selenium (μg/d)	60	40	-	15	n.a.	n.a.
Iodine (μg/d)	140	70	-	-	4	3

* only last trimester   ** 0-4 m, 4m+   *** based on protein providing 14.7% of EAR for energy   - = no reference value
n.a.= data not available   • an additional periconceptual supplement of 400μg is also advised (see para 4.3.1)

4.4.2   Current practice

There are no national data on dietary intakes during pregnancy because pregnant women were not included in the National Dietary and Nutritional Survey of British Adults. A review of studies conducted among local populations within the UK is reported in Table 33. Supplement consumption during pregnancy has also been recorded in the quinquennial Infant Feeding Surveys: in 1995 62% of women reported taking supplements antenatally and 50% reported the use of folic acid supplements in early pregnancy. Of those who took supplements, 95% took iron and 25% took vitamins (Foster et al, 1997). The Infant Feeding Survey also reported that 66% of women drank alcohol during pregnancy, 70% of whom consumed <1 unit per week. A further 28% consumed 1-7 units a week and 3% consumed 8 units per week or more (Foster et al, 1997).

4.5   Lactation

4.5.1   Recommendations

Increments for energy and certain nutrients for lactating women are given in Table 4.1 and Table 4.2. Estimated Average Requirements (EAR) for lactation are calculated as increments to be added to the mother's EAR and are based on the

16

duration and intensity of breastfeeding. "Group 1" in table 4.1 includes mothers who "*practise exclusive or almost exclusive breastfeeding until the baby is 3-4 months old and then progressively introduce weaning foods as part of an active weaning process which often lasts only a few months*". "Group 2" mothers are those "*who introduce only limited complementary feeds after 3-4 months and whose intention is that breast milk should provide the primary source of nourishment for 6 months or more*". Increments for other nutrients are based on the nutrient content of breastmilk. The lactation increment of 10µg for vitamin D has been recently re-endorsed by COMA (Department of Health, 1998b).

There is no evidence of impaired lactational efficiency or detriment to the mother's health if the additional nutrients are not consumed and there is much evidence of physiological adaptations to achieve maternal energy efficiency (Prentice *et al*, 1996). In other words there is no evidence that breastfeeding is detrimental either to a mother's health or to her nutritional status. Moreover, a review of international data suggested that the efficiency of lactation is conserved even in the presence of severe undernutrition (Prentice & Prentice, 1995).

4.5.2   Current Practice
There are no national data on diet during lactation. Two small UK studies were conducted more than ten years ago (Black *et al*, 1986; Schofield *et al*, 1989).

4.6   **Infancy**

4.6.1   Recommendations

4.6.1.i   *Birth to 4-6 months*
"*The Panel endorsed human milk as best for babies and saw no value in setting the DRVs for breast-fed infants. The Panel therefore decided that DRVs would be set only for infants with artificial feeds (formulas)* (see Table 3 and Table 6) *whose nutrients are dependent on the composition of the artificial feeds being offered. For most nutrients the DRV of infants who are not wholly breastfed represents at least the same amount of each nutrient from the formulas and other foods as the wholly breastfed infant of the same age would receive*" (Department of Health, 1991).

In 1974, recommendations for the nutritional composition of breastmilk substitutes were first made to avoid the risks of hypernatraemic dehydration and hypocalcaemic tetany (DHSS, 1974). Subsequently the composition of infant formula has been legally defined in European Directives, enacted in the UK as the *Infant Formula and Follow-on Formula Regulations 1995* and subsequent amendment (1997) (Table 4.3). Subsequent amendments have permitted the addition of nucleotides and long chain polyunsaturated fatty acids (LCPUFAs). Not all UK formulas contain LCPUFAs. The COMA Panel on Child and Maternal Nutrition has previously considered whether these compounds should be regarded as an essential component of the diet of term infants. Despite limited data on differences in blood lipid profiles and brain fatty acid composition between breastfed and formula fed babies (Farquharson *et al*, 1992; Makrides, 1994)

Table 4.3: Compositional guidelines for infant and follow-on formula (per 100ml) (The Infant and Follow-on formula regulations, 1995)*

	Infant formula**	Follow-on formula**
Energy (kcal)	60-75	60-80
Protein (g)	1.2-1.95	1.5-2.9
Carbohydrate (g)	4.6-9.1	4.6-9.1
Fat (g)	2.1-4.2	2.1-4.2
Vitamin A (μg) RE	39-117	39-117
Vitamin D (μg)	0.65-1.63	0.65-1.95
Vitamin E (mg)	≥0.33	≥0.3
Vitamin K (μg)	2.6	Ns
Thiamin (μg)	26	Ns
Riboflavin (μg)	39	Ns
Niacin equiv (μg)	163	Ns
Vitamin B6 (μg)	22.8	Ns
Vitamin B12 (μg)	0.07	Ns
Total folate (μg)	2.6	Ns
Pantothenic acid (μg)	195	Ns
Biotin (μg)	1.0	Ns
Vitamin C (mg)	5.2	5.2
Sodium (mg)	13-39	Ns
Potassium (mg)	39-94	Ns
Chloride (mg)	32.5-81	Ns
Calcium (mg)	32.5	Ns
Phosphorus (mg)	16.3-58.5	Ns
Magnesium (mg)	3.3-9.8	Ns
Iron (μg)	325-975	650-1300
Copper (μg)	13-52	Ns
Zinc (μg)	325-975	325
Iodine (μg)	3.3	3.3

Ns= not specified   * one value only indicates minimum permissible value   **calculated for a product containing 65kcal/100ml

current data do not conclusively support differences in functional outcome between supplemented and unsupplemented infants who have been born at *term*. At present, therefore, we do not believe there is a compelling case for LCPUFA supplementation of infant formula, and we note that a recent American expert committee reached similar conclusions (Raiten *et al*, 1998).

The following recommendations concern foods other than breastmilk or infant formula for children aged under 6 months (Department of Health, 1994):

- *"Follow-on formula is not recommended as replacement for breastmilk or infant formula before six months"*. Indeed, even after 6 months COMA has not acknowledged a specific benefit associated with the use of follow-on formula as an alternative to breastmilk or infant formula.

Table 4.4: Infants: RNIs (Department of Health, 1991)

	0-3m	4-6m	7-9m	10-12m
Protein (g/d)	12.5	12.7	13.7	14.9
Thiamin (mg/d)	0.2	0.2	0.2	0.3
Riboflavin (mg/d)	0.4	0.4	0.4	0.4
Niacin (nicotinic acid equivalent mg/d)	3	3	4	5
Vitamin B6 (mg/d)	0.2*	0.2	0.3	0.4
Vitamin B12 (μg/d)	0.3	0.3	0.4	0.4
Folate (μg/d)	50	50	50	50
Vitamin C (mg/d)	25	25	25	25
Vitamin A (μg/d)	350	350	350	350
Vitamin D (μg/d)	8.5	8.5	7	7
Calcium (mg/d)	525	525	525	525
Phosphorus (mg/d)	400	400	400	400
Magnesium (mg/d)	55	60	75	80
Sodium (mg/d)	210	280	320	350
Potassium (mg/d)	800	850	700	700
Chloride (mg/d)	320	400	500	500
Iron (mg/d)	1.7	4.3	7.8	7.8
Zinc (mg/d)	4.0	4.0	5.0	5.0
Copper (mg/d)	0.2	0.3	0.3	0.3
Selenium (μg/d)	10	13	10	10
Iodine (μg/d)	50	60	60	60

* based on protein providing 14.7% of EAR for energy

- *The majority of infants should not be given solid foods before the age of four months, and a mixed diet should be offered by the age of six months.*

4.6.1.ii   4-6 months – one-year

The DRVs for children in this age group are listed in Table 4.1 and Table 4.4). Compositional requirements for the composition of follow-on formula are given in Table 4.3. Other key recommendations (Department of Health, 1994) are as follows:

- *From the age of six months, infants receiving breastmilk (or infant formula in quantities less than 500ml per day) as their main drink should be given supplements of vitamins A and D*

- *500-600 ml of breastmilk, infant formula or follow-on formula is given as a guideline volume for children aged 6-12 months*

- *Pasteurised whole cow's milk should only be used as a main milk drink after the age of one year*

Table 4.5: Children aged 1½-3½ years: DRVs and intakes

Nutrient	RNI (1-3y) (Department of Health, 1991)	LRNI (1-3y) (Department of Health, 1991)	%<LRNI (1½ -3½) (Gregory et al, 1995)
Protein (g)	14.5	-	-
Vitamin A (μg)	400	200	7-9
Thiamin (mg)	0.5	0.3	0-1
Riboflavin (mg)	0.6	0.3	0
Niacin (nic equiv) (mg)	8	5.3	0
Vitamin B6 (mg)*	0.7	0.5	1-2
Vitamin B12 (mg)	0.5	0.3	0
Folate (μg)	70	35	0
Vitamin C (mg)	30	8	1-2
Vitamin D (μg)	7	-	-
Calcium (mg)	350	200	1
Phosphorus (mg)	270	-	-
Magnesium (mg)	85	50	0-1
Sodium (mg)	500	200	0
Potassium (mg)	800	450	0
Chloride (mg)	800	-	-
Iron (mg)	6.9	3.7	12-24
Zinc (mg)	5.0	3.0	14-15
Copper (mg)	0.4	-	-
Iodine (μg)	70	40	3

- = no reference value set, * based on protein providing 14.7% of EAR for energy

4.6.2   Current practice

4.6.2.i   *Birth to 4-6 months*

The most recent national quinquennial Infant Feeding Survey indicated that in 1995, 66% of mothers initiated breastfeeding in the UK. Prevalence fell further with postnatal age to 43% at 6 weeks, 28% at 4 months, 21% at 6 months and 14% at 9 months (Foster *et al*, 1997). At 6-10 weeks only 21% of babies were *exclusively* breastfed and 62% were being exclusively formula fed. Amongst mothers not breastfeeding, 2% were giving follow-on formula as the main milk to babies aged 4-5 months.

The age at which solid foods were introduced also fell far short of recommendations. For the United Kingdom as a whole, 2% of babies had been fed solids by 4 weeks of age, 13% by 8 weeks, 56% by 3 months and 91% by four months (Foster *et al*, 1997). Thus only 10% of mothers deferred weaning until the recommended age of "..*at least 4 months*..".

4.6.2.ii   *4-6 months – one year*

The 1995 Infant Feeding Survey showed that only 27% of babies being breastfed at age 8-9 months were receiving vitamin supplements. Moreover, only 25% of those being fed cow's milk were receiving vitamins. The vitamins most frequently used were the Department of Health Children's Vitamin Drops which

Table 4.6: Children aged 3½-4½ years: DRVs and intakes

Nutrient	RNI (4-6y) (Department of Health, 1991)	LRNI (4-6y) (Department of Health, 1991)	%<LRNI (3½-4½) Gregory et al, 1995)
Protein (g/d)	19.7	-	-
Thiamin (mg/d)	0.7	0.4	0-2
Riboflavin (mg/d)	0.8	0.4	1
Niacin (nicotinic acid equivalent mg/d)	11	7.3	0
Vitamin B6 (mg/d)*	0.9	0.7	4
Vitamin B12 (μg/d)	0.8	0.5	0-1
Folate (μg/d)	100	50	0-1
Vitamin C (mg/d)	30	8	0-2
Vitamin A (μg/d)	400	200	7-8
Vitamin D (μg/d)	-	-	-
Calcium (mg/d)	450	275	2-3
Phosphorus (mg/d)	350	-	-
Magnesium (mg/d)	120	70	1-2
Sodium (mg/d)	700	280	0
Potassium (mg/d)	1100	600	1
Chloride (mg/d)	1100	-	-
Iron (mg/d)	6.1	3.3	4
Zinc (mg/d)	6.5	4.0	37-42
Copper (mg/d)	0.6	-	-
Iodine (μg/d)	100	50	6

- = no reference value set, * based on protein providing 14.7% of EAR for energy

were bought, received free or on prescription from the Child Health Clinic (see Section 3.1.1 and Table 3.1). Amongst mothers giving a non-human milk to their babies, only 1% were giving cow's milk at 4-5 months, but this increased to 16% by 8-9 months.

The 1986 nationally representative survey of the nutrient intakes of British infants aged 6-12 months showed that average intakes fell below RNI for only two nutrients: vitamin D (average intake 50% of RNI) and zinc (average intake 90% of RNI) (Mills & Tyler, 1992).

4.7   Young children

4.7.1   Recommendations
Table 4.1, Table 4.5 and Table 4.6 show the DRVs for young children. In addition to these the report on *Weaning and the Weaning Diet* (Department of Health, 1994) made the following recommendations:

- *The provision of adequate dietary energy to ensure normal growth and development should be a principal determinant of the diets of children under five years of age.*

- *Vitamin C in adequate amounts should be ensured to assist absorption of iron.*

21

- *For groups of children the average intake of non-milk extrinsic sugars should be limited to about ten per cent of total dietary energy intake.*

- *There should be adequate dietary intake of calcium.*

- *Continued use of iron-enriched infant formula or a follow-on milk as a main drink after the first year should be considered if there are concerns about the inadequacy of iron in the diet.*

- *Between the ages of one to five years, vitamins A and D supplements should be given unless adequate vitamin status can be assured from a diverse diet containing vitamins A and D rich foods and from moderate exposure to sunlight.*

- *Semi-skimmed milk should not be introduced until two years and skimmed until 5 years.*

A further important aspect of early childhood is the development of eating habits conducive to maintaining adequate nutritional intake. To this end the report *Weaning and the Weaning Diet* also included a food-based guide to weaning which recommended for a child at least a year old:

- *Milk (whole) and dairy products: minimum of 350ml milk per day or two servings of a dairy product. Large volumes (i.e. more than 600ml) should not be consumed as this may prevent appetite for other foods.*

- *Starchy foods: minimum of four servings (at least one at each mealtime). Discourage high fat foods such as crisps and pastry. Use wholemeal cereals where possible.*

- *Vegetables and Fruits: minimum of four servings. To improve iron absorption vegetables or unsweetened fruits should be given with every meal. If vegetables are refused they could be disguised in other foods.*

- *Meat and meat alternatives: minimum one serving daily or two from vegetable sources. Encourage low fat meat or oily fish. Use little or no extra fat.*

- *Occasional foods: limit crisps and savoury snacks. Give bread or fruit if hungry between meals. Do not add sugar to drink. Try to limit soft drinks to meal times.*

Fluoride drops for the prevention of caries are contraindicated in areas where the water supply contains more than 7 parts per million (ppm) of fluoride (whether naturally or added). Fluoride supplementation regimens have been recommended for children at high risk of caries who live in areas with water containing either <3ppm or 3-7ppm fluoride (British Dental Association *et al*, 1997). Fluoridation of water supplies is however regarded as the key public health measure for prevention of caries (section 7.2.4).

4.7.2   Current practice

Table 4.5 and Table 4.6 show the findings of the National Diet and Nutrition Survey (NDNS) of children aged 1½-4½ years. They show that average energy intake fell below the EAR for about 70% of children and that vitamin A (7-9% of children), iron (12-24% of children) and zinc (14-15% of children) intakes were those most likely to fall below LRNI. An LRNI is not set for vitamin D (most children will obtain vitamin D through sunlight exposure rather than diet) but almost 100% had intakes which fell short of RNI set for children up to 3 years of age. Approximately 10% of calcium intakes and one-third of vitamin C intakes fell below LRNI – nutrients identified by recommendations as being of particular importance. Only 12% of children in the survey had intakes of non-milk extrinsic sugars which contributed less than 10% of their dietary energy (Gregory *et al*, 1995). Approximately 20% of children consumed vitamin supplements, and about 40% of supplements consumed were vitamins A, C and D only (Gregory *et al*, 1995) (see section 5.6.2.ii).

4.8   **Schoolchildren & adolescents**

4.8.1   Recommendations

DRVs for children over the age of five years are shown in Table 4.7, Table 4.8 and Table 4.9. In addition to these, recommended upper limits for dietary fat intake also become relevant after the age of 5 years. The DRVs are expressed as a contribution to total dietary food energy and are as follows:

*   total fat – 35% (11% saturated fat),

*   non-milk extrinsic sugars – 11%,

*   intrinsic and milk sugars and starch – 39%.

The adult DRV for non-starch polysaccharides is 18g/day (Department of Health, 1991).

The Government has introduced Regulations on National Nutritional Standards for School Lunches. Guidance is food based rather than specifying nutrient contents. The Regulations should come into force in May 2002 though they are available for inclusion in new school meals contracts.

4.8.2   Current practice

Table 4.7 shows preliminary and unpublished data from the NDNS of young people aged 4 to 18 years. These indicate that zinc was the only nutrient for which some 7-10 year old children's intakes fell below the LRNI. For boys aged 11-14 years (Table 4.8) only intakes of calcium, magnesium and zinc fell below LRNI. However the girls in this age group had average intakes of iron and magnesium which fell below the RNI and at least a quarter had intakes of calcium and zinc

Table 4.7: School age children aged 7-10 years: DRVs and intakes

	RNI 7-10 y (Department of Health, 1991)	LRNI 7-10 y (Department of Health, 1991)	%<LRNI (NDNS unpublished data)	
			Girls	Boys
Protein (g/d)	28.3	-	-	-
Thiamin (mg/d)	0.7	0.4-0.45	0	-
Riboflavin (mg/d)	1.0	0.5	1	1
Niacin (nicotinic acid equivalent mg/d)	12	7.7-8.7	0	0
Vitamin B6 (mg/d) *	1.0	0.8	1	0
Vitamin B12 (µg/d)	1.0	0.6	1	0
Folate (µg/d)	150	75	2	0
Vitamin C (mg/d)	30	8	0	0
Vitamin A (µg/d)	500	250	9	9
Vitamin D (µg/d)	-	-	-	-
Calcium (mg/d)	550	325	5	2
Phosphorus (mg/d)	450	250	0	0
Magnesium (mg/d)	200	115	5	2
Sodium (mg/d)	1200	350	0	0
Potassium (mg/d)	2000	950	1	0
Chloride (mg/d)	1800	532	0	0
Iron (mg/d)	8.7	4.7	3	1
Zinc (mg/d)	7.0	4.0	10	5
Copper (mg/d)	0.7	-	-	-
Iodine (µg/d)	110	55	3	1

- = no reference value set, * based on protein providing 14.7% of EAR for energy

below LRNI. Their vitamin A, iodine and potassium intakes were also low. Similarly, more 15-18 year-old girls showed iron, magnesium, calcium, potassium and riboflavin intakes short of LRNI than boys (Table 4.9). In contrast to the recommendation that no more than 11% of food energy should be contributed by saturated fat, mean intakes contributed 13.8-15.3% of food energy across the age groups studied and a further 15.8-17.6% of food energy was contributed by non-milk extrinsic sugars.

The Health Survey for England (1995-7) reported activity levels among young people aged 2-15 years. As children got older they spent less time on physical activities and more time on sedentary activities such as watching television or doing homework. This was particularly marked for girls from age 12 upwards, a majority of whom were in the least active group (active for 30 minutes or less on five days in the previous week) (Prescott-Clark & Primatesta, 1998).

4.9   Conclusions

By comparing recommendations with dietary practices and nutrient intakes we have identified a number of nutritional "vulnerabilities" at population level across the age range from conception to adolescence. The major ones are as follows:

Table 4.8: School age children 11-14 years: DRVs and intakes

	RNI 11-14y (Department of Health, 1991)		LRNI 11-14y (Department of Health, 1991)		% <LRNI 11-14y (NDNS unpublished data)	
	Girls	Boys	Girls	Boys	Girls	Boys
Protein (g/d)	41.2	42.1	-	-	-	-
Thiamin (mg/d)	0.7	0.9	0.42	0.51	1	0
Riboflavin (mg/d)	1.1	1.2	0.8	0.8	22	6
Niacin (nicotinic acid equivalent mg/d)	12	15	8.1	9.8	0	0
Vitamin B6 (mg/d) *	1.0	1.2	0.8	0.9	1	1
Vitamin B12 (µg/d)	1.2	1.2	0.8	0.8	1	0
Folate (µg/d)	200	200	100	100	3	1
Vitamin C (mg/d)	35	35	9	9	1	0
Vitamin A (µg/d)	600	600	250	250	20	12
Vitamin D (µg/d)	-	-	-	-	-	-
Calcium (mg/d)	800	1000	450	480	24	12
Phosphorus (mg/d)	625	775	345	365	0	0
Magnesium (mg/d)	280	280	180	180	51	28
Sodium (mg/d)	1600	1600	460	460	0	0
Potassium (mg/d)	3100	3100	1600	1600	19	10
Chloride (mg/d)	2500	2500	710	710	0	0
Iron (mg/d)	14.8	11.3	8.0	6.1	44	3
Zinc (mg/d)	9.0	9.0	5.3	5.3	37	14
Copper (mg/d)	0.8	0.8	-	-	-	-
Iodine (µg/d)	130	130	65	65	13	3

- = no reference value set   * based on protein providing 14.7% of EAR for energy

- Low dietary intake of folate among women of reproductive age (section 4.3.2).

- Low prevalence of breastfeeding (section 4.6.2.i).

- Unnecessarily early introduction of weaning foods (section 4.6.2.i).

- Low uptake of vitamin supplementation amongst pregnant and lactating women, and amongst babies >6 months who are breastfed or receiving cow's milk (sections 4.4.2 and 4.6.2.ii).

- Low intakes of certain micronutrients e.g. zinc, iron, and vitamin A amongst pre-school children (section 4.7.2).

- High intakes of non-milk extrinsic sugars among pre-school children (section 4.7.2).

- Low nutrient intakes (particularly iron, calcium and magnesium) amongst adolescent girls (section 4.8.2).

Table 4.9: School age children aged 15-18 years: DRVs and intakes

	RNI 15-18 years (Department of Health, 1991)		LRNI 15-18 years (Department of Health, 1991)		% <LRNI (NDNS unpublished data)	
	Girls	Boys	Girls	Boys	Girls	Boys
Protein (g/d)	45.0	55.2	-	-	-	-
Thiamin (mg/d)	0.8	1.1	0.49	0.63	2	0
Riboflavin (mg/d)	1.1	1.3	0.8	0.8	21	6
Niacin (nicotinic acid equivalent mg/d)	14	18	9.3	12.1	1	0
Vitamin B6 (mg/d) *	1.2	1.5	0.9	1.1	5	1
Vitamin B12 (µg/d)	1.5	1.5	1.0	1.0	2	0
Folate (µg/d)	200	200	100	100	4	0
Vitamin C (mg/d)	40	40	10	10	0	0
Vitamin A (µg/d)	600	700	250	300	12	12
Vitamin D (µg/d)	-	-	-	-	-	-
Calcium (mg/d)	800	1000	450	480	19	9
Phosphorus (mg/d)	625	775	345	366	1	0
Magnesium (mg/d)	300	300	190	190	53	18
Sodium (mg/d)	1600	1600	575	575	0	0
Potassium (mg/d)	3500	3500	2000	2000	38	15
Chloride (mg/d)	2500	2500	890	890	0	0
Iron (mg/d)	14.8	11.3	8.0	6.1	48	2
Zinc (mg/d)	7.0	9.5	4.0	5.5	10	9
Copper (mg/d)	1.0	1.0	-	-	-	-
Iodine (µg/d)	140	140	70	70	10	1

- = no reference value set   *based on protein providing 14.7% of EAR for energy

- Excessive intakes of saturated fat and non-milk extrinsic sugars amongst all school age children (section 4.8.2).

- Low levels of physical activity, particularly amongst adolescent girls (section 4.8.2).

It is important to recognise that these findings at population level mask considerable variation in behaviour between sub-groups and individuals. In the next chapter we try to identify the factors which account for this, in order to characterise those population sub-groups who are most nutritionally vulnerable.

Chapter 5: Identifying the nutritionally vulnerable

5.1 Terms of Reference

The Panel was asked *"To characterise any groups particularly vulnerable to nutritional inadequacy, and the vulnerabilities"*. In undertaking this task it is important first to acknowledge that the special nutrient demands and critical growth periods experienced by children and women of childbearing age *de facto* makes them nutritionally vulnerable (see chapter 1).

5.2 Assessing nutritional status

The term "nutritional status" is widely used to summarise the individual's position with respect to the maintenance of nutrient homeostasis. Broadly speaking, status can be assessed by reference to nutrient balance, body composition and metabolic function:

- *Energy and nutrient balance.* This can be estimated from measurements of nutrient intake (supply) and losses (demand). Most commonly assessment of intake is employed to approximate the adequacy of supply. At a population level such measurements can be set against DRVs to estimate the probability of deficiency arising (Department of Health, 1991).

- *Body composition.* Anthropometry is the simplest technique for assessing directly body composition and the most easily applicable to populations. Comparison of single or serial measurements against references (section 5.2.3) permits interpretation of the significance of inter-group differences in growth outcome. Sub-optimal growth is an important marker of nutritional vulnerability, particularly in infancy.

- *Metabolic function.* Variation in metabolic function across a population is marked at one extreme by enhanced (or "elite") performance and at the other by clinical signs of deficiency, disease or death. Reversible impairment of cognitive skills associated with iron deficiency constitutes an example of functional consequences of deficiency measurable in the child population.

A weakness of these methods of assessment is that to a large extent they quantify changes which have already occurred in the child as an outcome of sub-optimal nutrition. However, identifying groups with high prevalence of such markers allows them to be characterised as "nutritionally vulnerable".

5.2.1   Characterising the causes of "nutritional vulnerability"
Those at-risk can be identified not only by assessment of nutritional status but by recognition of predisposing factors. Identifying groups on this basis offers opportunities to intervene at several levels in order to erect a "safety net". The causes of nutritional vulnerability can be viewed as affecting individuals, households, or societies (see Figure 5.4). Adopting this approach sub-optimal early growth ("failure-to-thrive" section 5.5.3.i) can be viewed merely as the direct outcome of low nutrient intake beneath which a range of social and environmental factors contribute. For these reasons we have chosen to characterise "nutritional vulnerability" not only by considering nutritional status but also by taking into account the socio-economic and behavioural factors which place individuals at risk.

In this chapter we characterise nutritionally vulnerable groups by taking two approaches. Firstly, we consider growth as a summary measure of the influence of nutrition and other factors on health and development. Secondly, we take a life cycle perspective on common disorders of nutritional aetiology and attempt to identify population groups most at-risk.

5.2.2   Growth as an indicator of health and development
"Provided always that parental size is known, growth emerges as a primary measure of a child's physical and mental health. The study of growth emerges also as a powerful tool for monitoring the health and nutrition of populations, especially in ecological and economic circumstances that are sub-optimal. It can be used for studying the effect of political organisation upon the relative welfare of the various social, cultural and ethnic groups which make up a modern state. Thus the study of growth has a very direct bearing upon human welfare." (Tanner, 1989).

Three defined growth phases (infant, childhood and adolescent) with distinctive endocrine processes characterise the process of adult height attainment. The infant phase is particularly rapid and is nutritionally led. These factors account for the much greater vulnerability of young children to long-term effects of undernutrition such as stunting. Each of the phases is additive and the age at onset of each plays a critical role in determining final adult height (Karlberg *et al*, 1994). Final height is therefore the outcome of environmental and genetic factors acting from conception to adulthood. Growth may also reflect inter-generational processes leading to secular change as observed, for example, in successive generations of British Asian families (Chinn *et al*, 1998).

5.2.3   Growth references with which to judge nutritional status
Growth *references* are based on the growth patterns of representative samples of children in the general population. They are therefore descriptive rather than prescriptive and should not be confused with *standards* which represent patterns of optimal growth, or targets. The distinction is particularly relevant to assessing the growth of young infants. It is widely acknowledged that charts in current use do not accurately describe the true growth trajectory of infants exclusively

breastfed for about the first 6 months of life in accordance with WHO and other feeding recommendations (Rogers *et al*, 1997; Dewey *et al*, 1998).

In practice, four different sets of growth charts have been widely used in the United Kingdom:

- *"Tanner-Whitehouse 1965 charts"*. These are no longer in use.

- *"Tanner-Whitehouse 1976 Clinical Standards"* – a modification of the 1965 charts employing a longitudinal form. These also are no longer in widespread use.

- *"Buckler-Tanner 1995 charts"* – a modification to the 1976 charts. These are commonly used in hospitals.

- *British 1990 growth references ("Freeman charts")*. These are used more commonly in the community and were recommended by the Joint Working Party on Child Health Surveillance (Hall, 1996). First published in 1993 (Freeman *et al*, 1995), they are based on over twenty data sets collated in the 1980s and 1990s. The description "1990 charts" reflects the baseline year to which separate data sets were adjusted (Cole *et al*, 1998). They take a "nine-centile" form with channels spaced two-thirds of a standard deviation apart (0.4th, 2nd, 9th, 25th, 50th, 75th, 91st, 98th, 99.6th centiles) (Cole, 1994) and are published as "Four-in-one" charts by the Child Growth Foundation, London. It is worth noting that the data used in the first two years were collected in Cambridge where the prevalence of breastfeeding was relatively high.

5.2.4   Growth screening
Growth velocity is greatest in the first two years of life (Tanner, 1989) and growth achieved during this period forms the foundations for growth potential in later life. Monitoring the growth of infants and pre-school children has therefore become a key component of child health surveillance. The Joint Working Party on Child Health Surveillance recently indicated that whilst frequent weighing can provide useful reassurance, less frequent height measurements (three times between 18 months and 5 years and once between 7 and 9 years) are adequate for detecting abnormal growth (Hall, 1991; Hall, 1996). Others have pointed to a lack of evidence for the sensitivity of repeated height measurements given that height velocity is conditional on height and age (Mulligan *et al*, 1998; Voss, 1999). Thus a single measurement at five years to screen for "silent disease" has been favoured by some (Voss, 1999).

5.2.5   Vulnerable groups
Rates of growth during childhood vary between and within populations. Between 1972 and 1994 improvements in the standard of living for the British population as a whole have resulted in a secular trend to increased height demonstrated by the National Study of Health and Growth (NSHG) (Hughes *et al*, 1997) and a

decline in the age of menarche. Similar trends have been noted in Nordic countries (Brundtland *et al*, 1980). Beneath these secular trends lie differences between population groups which may reflect inequality at any one time – past or present. In developing countries, stunting has been regarded as a more sensitive and specific indicator of poverty than the more widely used composite indicators of socio-economic status. Thus while weight is more acutely affected by energy intake, height is an outcome of complex interactions between genetic potential and the environment. In Britain, adult height also shows a strong association with social deprivation and there is a difference of almost 2 cm between the mean heights of well-off and unskilled groups (Tanner, 1992). The prevalence of short stature among children is also higher among poorer population sub-groups (White *et al*, 1995).

In the NSHG the relationship between socio-economic factors and height in children aged 5 to 10 years was reduced to marginal significance after controlling for parental height (Rona & Chinn, 1995). In another, socio-economic factors remained significant independent contributors (Voss *et al*, 1998). It is important to recognise that intergenerational effects of low socio-economic status may affect both the parents' and their child's heights, a phenomenon labelled the "recycling of poverty" (Rona & Chinn, 1995). This perhaps calls into question the validity of controlling for parental height when studying such effects.

The NSHG has also demonstrated that height of primary schoolchildren varies between ethnic groups in the United Kingdom. Although secular trends to increasing height mirror those of representative British samples, the intergenerational catch-up of groups, such as the "other Indian" (mainly Bengali), Gujarati and Urdu/Punjabi children, has been insufficient to eradicate the height differences between groups (Chinn *et al*, 1998). Children of Asian origin remain on average shorter and thinner than white ones though Afro-Caribbean children are taller (see Figure 5.1 and Figure 5.2).

5.2.6   Conclusions

- Secular changes towards increasing height in British children are probably accountable to a number of environmental factors, not merely improvements in nutrition.

- Beneath these changes at population level, ethnic origin and socio-economic status continue to have independent effects on final adult height.

- Strategies directed towards increasing the mean height of vulnerable groups are likely to affect the height of subsequent generations.

Figure 5.1: Mean heights of boys (1993/4)[1]

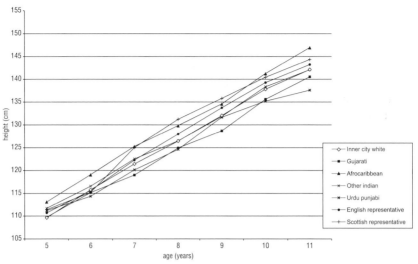

¹graph reproduced with kind permission from the author (Chinn *et al*, 1998).

Figure 5.2: Weight for height index for boys (1993/4)[2]

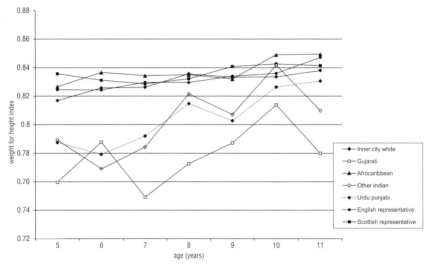

²graph reproduced with kind permission from the author (Chinn *et al*, 1998).

5.3 Conception

5.3.1 Neural tube defects

5.3.1.i *Numbers of affected pregnancies*

The association between maternal folate status and the development of fetal neural tube defects (NTD) is now well established (Department of Health, 2000). It has been estimated that daily supplementation with folic acid (pre- and peri-conceptionally – see section 4.3.1) could reduce the incidence of affected pregnancies by 50% (Department of Health, 2000). Other approaches could include food fortification, the risks and benefits of which have been recently reviewed (Department of Health, 2000).

5.3.1.ii *Who is at risk?*

Vulnerable groups can be identified on criteria of intake (from food and supplements), blood folate concentrations or incidence of neural tube defects (NTD).

- *Incidence.* Data on incidence suggest that a higher proportion of pregnancies are affected in Scotland and Northern Ireland than in England and Wales (Table 5.1) and that NTDs are slightly more likely to affect women from lower social class, and at the younger or older end of the reproductive age range (Department of Health, 1992).

- *Blood concentration.* The National Dietary and Nutritional Survey (NDNS) of British Adults indicated that approximately a quarter of non-pregnant British women aged 18-64 years in 1986-7 had low folate status (ascertained as red cell folate concentration <120µg/L[1]). Mean red cell folate concentrations decreased consistently with social class such that women in social classes IV and V had mean red cell folate concentrations about 30µg/L lower than those in social classes I and II (Gregory *et al*, 1990).

- *Intake.* Intake data confirmed that almost half of women aged 19-50 were consuming less than 50% of the RNI (200µg for non-pregnant women) (MAFF, 1994) (Table 5.21). National recommendations state that all women planning a pregnancy should consume about 600µg of folate per day from food and supplements (Department of Health, 1992). Prior to the 1992 recommendations the daily intakes of folate, including supplements, ranged from 235 µg per day for women in social classes I and II to 196 µg per day for women in social classes IV and V (Gregory *et al*, 1990). The 1997 National Food Survey supports this evidence of an income gradient in household availability of folate (MAFF, 1998).

A number of smaller localised dietary surveys among pregnant women have also indicated social class effects (see Table 5.21). In a 1980 survey of pregnant women living in a deprived East London community folate was the micronutrient most strongly negatively correlated with social class (categorised by husband's occupation or woman's occupation if single), though other potential confounders were not controlled for. This was attributed to lower consumption of fruit, vegetables and breakfast cereals (Wynn *et al*, 1994). Other studies have supported these findings (Eaton *et al*, 1984; Schofield *et al*, 1989; Rogers *et al*, 1998). After controlling for a range of potential confounders, Mathews *et al* showed that maternal age overrode the effects of social class on folate intakes and low maternal age was strongly associated with lower intakes of folate (Mathews *et al,* 2000).

---

[1] Impending folate deficiency is manifested by low serum folate and reduced folate stores (red cell folate <150µg/L) (FAO/WHO, 1988)

Table 5.1: NTD affected pregnancies in the United Kingdom

	England and Wales (1998[1])	Scotland (1997[2])	Northern Ireland (1998[3])
Number of live births	635,549	57,940	24,277
Number of NTD affected live births [4]:	**68**	**66**	**14***
Spina bifida	54**	}	
Anencephaly	8	}66	
Encephalocele	6	}	
Number of still births	3401	319	132
Number of NTD affected still births [4]:	**26**	**8**	
Spina bifida	9	}	
Anencephaly	14***	}8	
Encephalocele	3***	}	
Number of therapeutic abortions	177,871[5]	12,109[6]	-
Number of NTD effected therapeutic abortions [4]:	**305**	**59[7]**	-
Spina bifida	120	17	
Anencephaly	163	28	
Encephalocele	22	1	

* including still births   ** includes one child with spina bifida occulta
*** includes one child with anencephaly and encephalocele, – data not available
[1] (TSO, 1999a) [2] (ISD (Scotland) CSA, Edinburgh. unpublished data) [3] (DHSS, Northern Ireland unpublished data)
[4] (National Congenital Anomaly System) [5] (TSO, 1999b) [6] (Notification (to the Chief Medical Officer, SODoH) of abortions
performed under the Abortion Act 1967) [7] Includes hydrocephalus, craniorachischisis, holoprosencephaly, Arnold-Chiari
syndrome, and other congenital malformations of the spinal cord.

The 1992 Department of Health recommendations for folate intakes for pre- and peri-conceptional women indicated that amounts associated with prevention of NTD cannot be achieved through dietary measures alone and that supplements are required. A number of surveys have attempted to quantify compliance with this recommendation. The key findings (see Table 5.21) suggest wide variation in supplement consumption reflecting locality and year. Since new recommendations were made in 1992 uptake of supplements appears to have improved though it remains higher after conception than before. The 1995 Infant Feeding Survey based on retrospective *post partum* questioning of a national sample suggested that fifty percent had taken supplements in early pregnancy though it is unlikely that so many consumed them within the first 30 days of gestation when neural tube closure occurs. Knowledge of the folic acid recommendations was highest among women who were older on completing education and those from higher social classes (Foster *et al*, 1997).

Mathews *et al* (1998) have more recently shown that supplement consumption (pre- and peri-conceptional) is not only positively and independently associated with the woman's age and educational attainment but with cohabitation (only pre-conceptional supplements). It correlated negatively with smoking. These variables cancelled any effect of social class in multiple logistic regression.

The women least likely to take pre-conceptional folate supplements are those at greatest risk of unplanned pregnancies. A survey in 1989 indicated that 31% of pregnancies resulting in live births in England and Wales were unintended. The mothers involved were most likely to be single, young, to have two or more children, and to have completed full-time education before the age of 18 years (Fleissig, 1991).

A recent report has noted that the rates of teenage pregnancy in Great Britain are the highest in Europe. As three-quarters of these teenage pregnancies are unplanned (Social Exclusion Unit, 1999) pre-conceptional folic acid supplement uptake is likely to be minimal. The Social Exclusion Unit cited a 1979 study in which a quarter of teenage mothers first consulted their GP when more than 3 months pregnant suggesting that post-conceptional supplementation is also likely to be reduced among these women. A study of 16-19 year old women in 1996 showed that only 8-15% of women who were still in education or youth training knew that taking folic acid supplements before conception reduced the chances of having a baby with spina bifida. Older women of higher social class were more likely to know about supplements (Wild *et al*, 1996).

5.3.1.iii *Conclusions*

- The preventable proportion of neural tube defects is greatest in those of lowest socio-economic status, probably because they eat less dietary folate than the more affluent.

- Supplement consumption is lowest among less well-educated, single and younger women who smoke.

- The women least likely to take folic acid supplements are those most likely to have an unplanned pregnancy

5.4   **Pregnancy and lactation**

It is important to recognise that adequate pre-conceptual nutrition during teenage years is crucial in the preparation for reproduction (sections 3.1; 4.8.1; 5.4.5). This probably applies as much to micronutrient as to macronutrient status. Current limitations in the assessment of micronutrient status particularly constrain analysis of the relationship between low maternal intakes and pregnancy outcome.

5.4.1   Low Birth Weight

5.4.1.i   *Prevalence*
In England and Wales, 7.1% of live births were low birthweight (LBW; birthweight less than 2500g) (ONS, 1999a) compared to 6.8% in Scotland (ISD Scotland (SMR02), 1998) and 5.8% in Northern Ireland (DHSS Northern Ireland, 1998, unpublished data). LBW is frequently attributable to preterm birth and intrauterine growth retardation, which are not mutually exclusive[1]. Whatever its cause, LBW is associated with increased perinatal mortality and morbidity, the

---

[1] Intrauterine growth retardation is only one cause of low birth weight (<2500g). It may also be attributable to premature birth or fetal abnormality. A few babies of naturally small constitution may also weigh less than 2500g at birth. In some cases impaired uterine nutrition (i.e. growth retardation) is associated with birth weight above 2500g.

34

risk of mortality rising with increasing prematurity. Sub-optimal fetal growth is also associated with reduced postnatal growth and an increased risk of adult disease (Barker *et al*, 1993; Goldberg *et al*, 1994), particularly ischaemic heart disease, stroke and non insulin-dependent diabetes mellitus.

5.4.1.ii *The role of nutrition*

Although it has been argued that maternal nutrition during pregnancy has an important effect on fetal growth (Barker, 1992) evidence of a relationship in generally well-nourished populations like that of the UK is inconclusive (Haste, 1991; Godfrey *et al*, 1996; Mathews *et al*, 1999). Smoking and high alcohol intake are probably more important environmental causes of fetal growth constraint in such circumstances. Observational studies of the relationship between dietary intake and birth outcome in large groups of British pregnant women have reported inconsistent findings after controlling for major confounders such as maternal height, weight and smoking behaviour (Meis *et al*, 1997). This may reflect discrepancies in methods of dietary assessment. Godfrey *et al* (1996), using food frequency questionnaires, showed that high intakes of carbohydrate in early pregnancy and low intakes of animal protein in late pregnancy were associated with lower birth weight. Mathews *et al* (1999), using food diaries to record intake, found vitamin C the only nutrient independently associated with birth weight. However the size of effect did not appear to be of clinical importance. Haste *et al* (1991) showed that protein, zinc, thiamin and riboflavin intakes (assessed from weighed dietary intakes) were independently and positively associated with birth weight, accounting for 2-3% of the variance ($p<0.05$).

More direct evidence of any causal link between maternal nutritional status and birth weight can be obtained from randomised controlled trials of supplementation during pregnancy. A recent review concluded that balanced supplementation with energy and protein[1] was associated with increases in maternal weight gain and mean birth weight and a marginally significant decrease in the number of small-for-gestational age babies (de Onis *et al*, 1998). However the majority of the studies included were conducted in developing countries. Intervention studies in the UK have failed to demonstrate an effect on birthweight attributable to protein: energy supplementation during pregnancy (e.g. Viegas *et al*, 1982a; Doyle *et al*, 1992). One study of selected nutritionally "at risk" Asian mothers did show a positive effect (Viegas *et al*, 1982b) but failed to control for social class.

Randomised controlled trials of supplementation with micronutrients and fatty acids have also been reviewed (de Onis *et al*, 1998). Evidence was inconclusive but it was suggested that zinc, folate and magnesium supplementation warrant further research. Another review has similarly remarked upon zinc (Mathews, 1996) but for other nutrients (including vitamin D, iron, calcium and fatty acids) evidence of effect in white populations is inconsistent or absent. More recently, medicinal doses of vitamins C and E demonstrated a statistically significant

---

[1] a supplement where protein accounts for <25% of total energy content

reduction in the incidence of proteinuric hypertension associated with favourable changes in the plasminogen activator inhibitor (PAI1/PAI2) ratio for women at high risk of pre-eclampsia though this is the only study of its kind (Chappell *et al*, 1999).

In summary, the relationship between dietary factors during pregnancy outcome and birth weight are not strong. However, preliminary data suggest that certain measures of metabolic function may be more predictive than those of diet or body composition. For example, one study indicated that 23% of variability in birth length can be explained by variation in protein synthesis rates in the mother which were directly related to her visceral lean mass (Duggleby & Jackson 1999). More sensitive measures of the relationships between diet and pregnancy outcome may emerge.

5.4.1.iii *Who is at risk of low dietary intake during pregnancy?*
Ten studies have examined the average dietary intake of pregnant women. Table 5.22 highlights in shaded cells the average nutrient intakes which fell short of Dietary Reference Values (DRV). Only one study includes intake from dietary supplements (Mathews & Neil, 1998). Average intakes most likely to fall below DRV included energy (78-100% EAR), potassium (51-97% RNI), magnesium (81-115% RNI), iron (57-118% RNI), vitamin B6 (81-140% RNI), folate (19-56% RNI for early pregnancy), vitamin C (82-200% RNI) and vitamin D (9-43% RNI). Average intakes of vitamin A (currently included in the vitamin supplement provided by the Welfare Food Scheme) generally exceeded RNI, sometimes by several fold.

Four studies in the UK have examined maternal characteristics associated with dietary intake in pregnancy. Three (Wynn *et al*, 1994; Mathews *et al*; Rogers *et al*, 1998b) used an indicator of deprivation (social class and "difficulty in affording food" score respectively). Rogers *et al* and Wynn *et al* showed that, independent of smoking status, poorer people had lower nutrient intakes though no adjustment was made for maternal age. Rogers *et al* examined the intake of twenty nutrients and found that only three – calcium, vitamin E and riboflavin – were unaffected by financial difficulty. Mathews (personal communication) found that social class was an independent predictor of vitamin B1, vitamin B12, iron, vitamin C and vitamin D intake after controlling for height, smoking and age. However, once further adjustment was made for educational attainment, only vitamin C intake remained significant. Maternal age had the strongest effect on all intakes examined, with older women having significantly higher intakes of most nutrients (Mathews *et al*, 2000). This was attributed to the greater total food consumption and the higher nutrient densities of their diets.

Several studies have found smoking to be independently associated with nutrient intakes during pregnancy (Haste *et al*, 1991, and Rogers *et al*, 1998b) and relationships with a large range of micronutrients were noted. These studies did not control for age. After controlling for this, Mathews *et al* (2000) found that smoking was significantly and independently associated with reduced intakes of carotenoids and vitamin C.

Most UK studies of diet in pregnancy have not considered alcohol consumption though the 1995 Infant Feeding Survey showed that younger women were less likely either to drink alcohol during pregnancy or consume volumes which presented a risk. Of all those who drank during pregnancy 25% of those aged under 20 years consumed 1-7 units per week compared to 35% of those aged over 35 years (Foster *et al*, 1997).

5.4.1.iv *Conclusions*

• Observational data show that average nutrient intakes of pregnant women fall short of DRVs for a number of nutrients including energy, potassium, magnesium, iron, vitamin B6, folate and vitamins C and D.

• Low intakes of energy (and possibly zinc, magnesium and folate) have been linked speculatively to the aetiology of low birth weight though intervention studies have not confirmed causal relationships.

• Poor, younger women and those who smoke show the lowest intakes of nutrients but the extent to which nutritional factors explain the recognised strong associations between low birth weight and social class (Table 5.2) is unclear.

• There is no evidence that pregnant women in the UK have low vitamin A status. In practice intakes may exceed RNI several fold. This suggests that the inclusion of vitamin A in the Welfare Food Scheme vitamin supplements for pregnant women is at best unnecessary.

Table 5.2 : Prevalence of low birth weight according to social class in Great Britain in 1996

Social class categories used in England and Wales	% all live births which were LBW (<2500g) in England and Wales, 1997 (ONS, 1999a)	deprivation category used in Scotland (7= most deprived)	% all singleton live births which were LBW in Scotland, 1996 (ISD Scotland, 1998)
I	6.1	1	3.6
II	6.3	2	4.1
IIIN	6.4	3	4.8
IIIM	7.6	4	5.4
IV	8.0	5	6.2
V	8.4	6	6.2
Other	8.2	7	8.6

5.4.2   Iron deficiency anaemia

5.4.2.i *Prevalence*

There are no national data on the prevalence of iron deficiency in pregnancy. Moreover, there are some problems of definitions. WHO defines an anaemia in

37

pregnancy as a haemoglobin level of <11.0g/L (rather than 120g/L). This lower value reflects the fall attributable to the physiological haemodilution during pregnancy. Where non-pregnant women of childbearing age are concerned the National Dietary and Nutritional Survey of British adults (18-64 years) showed that 6% of women aged 18-24 years and 4% of those between 25 and 49 years had haemoglobin concentrations of 11.0g /dl or less. Among women aged 18-34, 13% had serum ferritin concentrations below 13μg/L, compatible with depletion of iron stores (Gregory *et al*, 1990).

Three studies which have reported the prevalence of anaemia in pregnancy in parts of England & Wales (see Table 5.3) suggest that severe anaemia affects few pregnant women.

Table 5.3: Prevalence of anaemia (measured by low haemoglobin concentration) in studies of pregnant women conducted in the UK

Author	Time period and location of study	Cut-off used (g/dl)	Gestational age at measurement (weeks)	% prevalence of anaemia
Robinson *et al*, 1998	1991-2 Southampton	<11.0	14	6
Godfrey *et al*, 1991	1987-9 Oxford	≤9.9 9.9-10.9	Lowest measurement obtained at any stage of pregnancy	9 28
Murphy *et al*, 1986	1970-79 Wales	<10.4	< 13	2.1

5.4.2.ii *The role of nutrition*
Table 5.22 shows that average iron intakes were consistently below RNI in local studies of pregnant women. Robinson *et al* (1998) found that dietary intake of iron had no correlation with several measures of iron status after controlling for confounders (Robinson *et al*, 1998). In this observational study, calcium intake was associated with lower and alcohol with higher serum ferritin concentration but neither was related to haemoglobin concentration or mean red cell volume. The authors concluded that higher intakes of calcium in early pregnancy result at least in the short term in lower iron stores, possibly by reducing iron absorption (Robinson *et al*, 1998).

Consumption of iron supplements during pregnancy has been measured in three large studies (Foster *et al*; 1997, Rogers *et al*, 1998a, 1998b; Mathews & Neil, 1998):

• In the 1995 Infant Feeding Survey 62% of women questioned postnatally reported taking supplements during pregnancy, and 95% of these took iron. A higher proportion of mothers in Northern Ireland (85%) reported taking supplements (Foster *et al*, 1997).

• In the ALSPAC study of a cohort in Avon, SW England 43% of women were consuming iron supplements at 32 weeks gestation (Rogers *et al*, 1998a).

• In a Portsmouth study, only 7.8% were taking iron supplements at 12 weeks gestation (Mathews & Neil, 1998). This low uptake probably reflects early ascertainment as Rogers *et al* (1998a) reported that supplement use increased in later pregnancy.

None of the studies demonstrated a significant correlation with socio-economic indicators though Rogers *et al* (1998b) noted that smokers were more likely to take supplements.

5.4.2.iii *Consequences of iron deficiency anaemia in pregnancy*
Most of the reported adverse effects of iron deficiency are unsubstantiated by supplementation trials. Severe anaemia has been associated with increased maternal mortality and iron deficiency has been linked to low birth weight and prematurity but a causal relationship has not been conclusively demonstrated. Similarly there is little evidence to suggest that the iron stores of the newborn are affected by the mother's iron status (Allen, 1997).

5.4.2.iv *Who is at risk?*
Four studies have confirmed an association between low iron status and social class (Murphy *et al*, 1986; Godfrey *et al*, 1991; Robinson *et al*, 1998; Mathews, personal communication). Godfrey *et al* (1991) reported that haemoglobin concentrations <9.9g/dl occurred among 12% of pregnant women in classes IV and V, 10% of those in social class III and 7% of those in classes I and II. Mathews (personal communication) showed that the correlation between social class and haemoglobin concentration was evident at 16 weeks but not at 30 weeks gestation. Relationships have also been shown between haemoglobin levels and ethnicity. A study in a multiethnic community in Birmingham reported statistically significant differences in mean haemoglobin concentration between pregnant European (12.6 g/dl), Asian (12.2 g /dl) and Afro-Caribbean (11.9 g/dl) women (Perry *et al*, 1995).

5.4.2.v *Conclusions*

- Iron deficiency anaemia in pregnancy affects a small proportion of women though severe anaemia is rare.

- There is a graded association of anaemia with social class such that women in social classes IV and V are most likely to be affected as well as women in ethnic minority groups.

- Although iron intake is frequently below DRV, there is little correlation between iron intake and iron status as measured by haemoglobin.

- One study has demonstrated an inverse association between serum ferritin concentration and calcium intake in early pregnancy.

- The consequences of iron deficiency anaemia in pregnancy in the UK are not well documented.

5.4.3   Bone Health

5.4.3.i   *Calcium balance during pregnancy and lactation.*

Mineralisation of the fetal skeleton principally occurs in the last trimester when calcium is deposited at a rate of 200-250mg per day. During lactation a similar quantity of calcium is transferred from the mother to the baby *via* breastmilk (Prentice *et al*, 2000). Recent research suggests that these additional calcium demands are met by adaptive changes which include increased absorption of dietary calcium, alterations in renal tubular reabsorption of calcium, and mobilisation of maternal bone with subsequent repletion at weaning (Prentice *et al*, 2000). There is no conclusive evidence that these changes increase long term risk of osteoporosis and fractures (Prentice *et al*, 2000), nor evidence that increasing dietary calcium intake during pregnancy and lactation attenuates maternal bone loss (Department of Health, 1998b). Studies of calcium supplementation during lactation have shown no effect on bone mineral content amongst women with either lower (Prentice *et al*, 1995) or higher calcium intakes (Kalkwarf, 1997).

Table 5.22 shows typical calcium intakes during pregnancy in the UK: none of the average intakes is below the RNI. Two studies during lactation (Black *et al*, 1986; Schofield *et al*, 1989) observed average daily intakes between 673-1500mg. The RNI for lactating women (aged 19-50) is 1250mg per day, including an increment for lactation of 550mg. UK and USA DRVs take further account of the demands for growth among pregnant or breastfeeding adolescents, but evidence that lower intakes are detrimental to the mother or her baby is again controversial. The effect of adolescent pregnancy and lactation on final adult stature or bone mass has not been studied (Prentice A, personal communication). Despite the paucity of evidence, DRV increments for pregnancy and lactation continue to form a part of current recommendations (Department of Health, 1998b).

5.4.3.ii   *Conclusions.*

- Limited data suggest that average calcium intakes of pregnant and breastfeeding women in the UK approximate or exceed the RNI.

- Calcium demands associated with mineralisation of the fetal and infant skeleton are met by adaptive changes in the mother which include mobilisation of bone mineral.

- There is no evidence that calcium supplementation during pregnancy or lactation attenuates this process.

- There is no evidence that low calcium intake is detrimental to the mother's long term skeletal health.

5.4.4   Vitamin D deficiency

5.4.4.i   *Prevalence*

There are no national data on plasma 25-hydroxyvitamin D levels for pregnant and lactating women. Average intakes of vitamin D were consistently lower than

RNI during pregnancy (Table 5.22). Usually most of the vitamin D needed is obtained through exposure to the sun.

5.4.4.ii *Who is at risk?*

Although there are no national data, Asian pregnant women seem to be particularly vulnerable to vitamin D deficiency. Especially low intakes were apparent in studies of Asian women (Eaton *et al*, 1984; Abraham *et al*, 1987; Table 33). In addition, a study conducted in Wales showed that serum parathyroid hormone (PTH) concentrations were significantly higher among Asian than Caucasian women, both during early pregnancy and at delivery (Alfaham *et al*, 1995). Vitamin D deficiency measured by serum 25-Hydroxyvitamin D has also been noted among Asian pregnant women elsewhere in Great Britain (Brooke *et al*, 1980; Ong *et al*, 1983).

Table 5.4 shows the proportions of pregnant and breastfeeding women who reported consuming vitamin supplements. Antenatal consumption data are not available for Asian women although, compared to white controls, more reported supplement consumption in the early weeks of breastfeeding. This differential was not maintained 4-5 months after delivery. The 1995 Infant Feeding Survey indicated that women of higher social class were more likely to take supplements both ante- and post-natally (Foster *et al*, 1997) but it is not known whether this applies to Asian women.

Table 5.4: Dietary supplement use during pregnancy and lactation

Recipient of supplement	% General population (Foster *et al*, 1997 and Gregory *et al*, 1995)	% Bangladeshi	% Pakistani	% Indian	% White
		(Thomas & Avery, 1997)			
Antenatal women (retrospectively)	25*	NA	NA	NA	NA
Breastfeeding mothers 6-10 weeks post partum	31	43	41	40	31
Breastfeeding mothers 4-5 months post partum	26	19	21	27	32

NA= not available   *includes only vitamin supplements

5.4.4.iii *Conclusions*

• Vitamin D deficiency has been noted in local populations of Asian pregnant women.

• Supplements are likely to form an important safety net during pregnancy though many Asian women, a high risk group, do not consume them.

5.4.5   Maternal body size

5.4.5.i *Prevalence*

Maternal height, maternal weight and weight gain during pregnancy are the measures which most strongly correlate with birth weight. This emphasises the particular problems associated with pregnancy during teenage years before the attainment of final adult weight. In these circumstances weight for height is likely to be lower than in older age groups, which may have important implications for long-term fetal health outcome (Fall *et al*, 1999; Godfrey *et al*, 1999).

5.4.5.ii *Obesity*

Obesity is associated with an increased risk of maternal complications (including pregnancy–induced hypertension, gestational diabetes mellitus and caesarian delivery), congenital malformations (particularly neural tube defects) and peri-natal death (Prentice & Goldberg, 1996; Edwards *et al*, 1996; de Groot *et al*, 1999). The risk appears unrelated to dietary intake during pregnancy and does not result from associated dietary deficiency (Prentice & Goldberg, 1996). Those obese women who do show large weight gains are more likely to give birth to large-for-gestational-age babies and are less likely to return to their pre-pregnant weight (Zhou & Olsen, 1997). There is some evidence that the risk to the fetus associated with excess maternal weight in pregnancy is greater among short than tall women (Forsen *et al*, 1997).

5.5   **Infancy**

5.5.1   Breastfeeding

5.5.1.i   *Benefits for mother and baby*

Breastmilk constitutes the reference diet of the young infant (Department of Health, 1991; Department of Health, 1996; section 4.6.1.i). Breastfed babies are less likely to become ill than those who are bottle-fed (British Paediatric Association, 1994; Heinig & Dewey, 1997; Golding *et al*, 1997a,b). A prospective cohort study in Dundee, Scotland, showed that gastro-intestinal illness occurred significantly less frequently in infants breastfed for 13 weeks or more than in those bottle-fed, even after adjustment for confounding factors (Howie *et al*, 1990). A dose-response relationship was apparent amongst those partially breastfed and there was evidence of continued protection throughout the first year of life. Others have reported significant reductions in the risk of otitis media, upper and lower respiratory tract infections, wheezing, *Haemophilus influenzae* B meningitis, and necrotising enterocolitis (Golding *et al*, 1997). The strong influence of socio-economic factors on patterns of infant feeding in the UK poses some problems in demonstrating a causal link (Bauchner *et al*, 1986; Golding *et al*, 1997b).

Breastfeeding is also associated with improved long-term health outcome. Follow-up of the Dundee cohort (*vide supra*) at the age of 7 years showed that exclusive breastfeeding was associated with significantly reduced risk of respiratory illness and wheezing during early childhood, whereas formula feeding was associated with higher systolic blood pressure (Wilson *et al*, 1998). A statistically significant association between the duration of exclusive breastfeeding and wheezing has also been noted in an Australian cohort of children followed to 6 years of age (Oddy *et al*, 1999). Breastfed babies also seem less likely to become overweight as children (von Kries *et al*, 1999). Advantages in long-term mental development attributable to breastfeeding have been reported in both pre-term and term infants, though controlling for the numerous confounding factors such as parenting skills and parental IQ is particularly difficult in this context (Florey *et al*, 1995; Golding *et al* 1997d).

Breastfeeding is also advantageous for maternal health. The majority of studies have shown a significant association between duration of lactation and post-pregnancy weight loss. The balance of evidence suggests that extended lactation is associated with reduced risk of premenopausal breast, ovarian and endometrial cancers though there is some controversy related to study design and other methodological factors (Heinig & Dewey, 1997).

The Department of Health estimated the cost savings to the NHS from the reduced incidence of gastro-enteritis attributable to breastfeeding to amount to £35 million in 1995 if all babies were breastfed (National Breastfeeding Working Group, 1995). Calculations have recently been published (Ball & Wright, 1999) for health service cost savings in the United States if all children were breastfed. Data were used for the frequency of health service utilisation for gastro-enteritis (drawn from a Scottish data set), lower respiratory tract illness and otitis media. Costs per never breastfed baby in the United States were estimated to be between $331-$475 during the first year of life.

5.5.1.ii *Who is at risk?*
Infant feeding practices are strongly influenced by country, social class, mother's age, parental educational attainment, smoking habit and ethnicity. The magnitude of these effects has been consistently demonstrated in the national quinquennial studies of infant feeding. Table 5.5 shows data collected in 1995 on the incidence[1] of breastfeeding.

In summary;

- In England and Wales, 68% of mothers initiated breastfeeding compared to 55% in Scotland and 45% in Northern Ireland (Foster *et al*, 1997).

- Asian mothers are more likely than white mothers to initiate breastfeeding (89-94% for first time mothers; Thomas & Avery, 1997) though there are no national data for other ethnic groups.

- Mothers who were significantly more likely to initiate breastfeeding for their first baby:

  - were older (>20-years) (England & Wales and Scotland)

  - had been educated longer (England & Wales, Scotland and Northern Ireland)

---

[1] that is the proportion of all births put to the breast after delivery

- were in social classes I or II (England & Wales and Northern Ireland)

- had been breastfed themselves (England & Wales, Scotland and Northern Ireland)

- had friends who breastfed (England & Wales, Scotland and Northern Ireland)

- did not smoke during pregnancy (England & Wales)

- held their babies immediately after delivery (England & Wales)

- In the case of mothers having second or subsequent babies, previous experience of breastfeeding and attendance at infant feeding classes significantly affected breastfeeding initiation.

- Continuing breastfeeding beyond two weeks was associated with similar factors to those involved with initiation.

Table 5.5: Percentage of mothers who initiate breastfeeding (Thomas & Avery, 1997; Foster *et al*, 1997)

	England and Wales	Scotland	Northern Ireland	United Kingdom
Total	68	55	45	66
Social class of husband / partner				
I	91	82	79	90
II	82	71	59	81
IIINM	72	65	55	71
IIIM	65	52	41	63
IV	58	48	38	57
V	50	56	36	50
Unclassified	62	56	33	61
No partner	49	30	24	46
Age at which mother completed education				
16 or under	53	39	26	51
17 or 18	74	59	46	72
Over 18	90	80	68	88
Age of mother				
Under 20	46	24	24	43
20-24	57	43	34	55
25-29	68	55	46	66
30 or over	76	65	50	74
Ethnicity				
White	62	NA	NA	NA
Bangladeshi	90			
Pakistani	76			
Indian	82			

NA = data not available

Table 5.6: Prevalence of breastfeeding at various ages (Thomas & Avery, 1997; Foster et al, 1997)

	Birth	1 week	6 weeks	4 months	6 months	9 months
Social class						
I	90	84	73	56	42	31
II	82	72	59	41	31	19
IIINM	72	64	48	30	23	18
IIIM	64	52	36	21	16	10
IV	57	46	33	21	17	11
V	50	40	23	13	11	5
No partner	47	37	25	13	9	6
Unclassified	62	54	38	25	19	14
Age at which mother completed education						
16 or under	52	41	27	16	12	8
17 or 18	72	62	45	27	19	10
Over 18	89	83	74	56	45	31
Ethnicity						
White	62	59	39	21	15	8
Bangladeshi	90	73	49	21	14	9
Pakistani	76	56	37	15	10	8
Indian	82	68	52	25	18	11

Table 5.6 shows the prevalence[1] of breastfeeding at various stages after birth. The proportion of women breastfeeding falls rapidly in all social classes and maternal educational categories, but it falls most rapidly amongst those who completed their education earlier and those in lower social classes. The most marked contrast is between Asian and white women: despite the higher incidence among Asian mothers the decline in prevalence is much more rapid. A small study of Afro-Caribbean mothers in Birmingham noted a high likelihood of initiation (91%) which fell to 64% at 4 weeks but then declined less rapidly to 24% at 6 months (Kemm et al, 1986). Amongst these women employment status and maternal age were not significantly associated with breastfeeding though women under 18 years were excluded.

5.5.1.iii Conclusions

- Breastmilk constitutes the reference diet of the young infant. The breastfed baby is a reference against which to judge nutritional and health outcomes achieved with artificial diets.

- Babies who are not breastfed are more likely to develop infection and be hospitalised in the first year of life.

- UK country of residence, social class, maternal educational attainment, smoking behaviour and ethnic background strongly influence mothers' choice of infant feeding method.

- Babies of young mothers in social classes IV and V who smoke and have been educated for shorter periods are those most likely to be disadvantaged.

---

[1] that is the proportion of all women giving any breastmilk at each stage after delivery

5.5.2 Introduction of complementary foods

5.5.2.i *Consequences of early introduction of solids*

It is currently recommended that all complementary foods including solids should not be introduced into the child's diet before the age of 4 months and not later than 6 months (section 4.6.1.i). Earlier introduction of solids has been associated with an increased probability of wheezing during childhood and an increased percentage body fat and weight at 7 years of age (Wilson *et al*, 1998).

5.5.2.ii *Who is at risk?*

The 1995 Infant Feeding Survey showed that timing of introduction of solid foods was positively associated with higher birth weight, bottle-feeding and social class. At three months, 35% of mothers in social class I had given solid food compared to 68% of mothers in social class V and 69% among mothers with no partner (Foster *et al*, 1997).

5.5.3 Failure to thrive

5.5.3.i *Definition*

Estimates of the prevalence of "failure to thrive" (FTT) are limited to local populations. Differences in definition may partly account for variation in prevalence. Table 5.7 shows definitions used in a number of UK community-based studies. Higher prevalences of malnutrition have been observed amongst children admitted to hospital: Hendrichse *et al* (1997) found that 26% of children aged 7-24 months admitted over a 2 month period to a hospital in Scotland were below 5th weight centile for age on Tanner and Whitehouse Standards.

Table 5.7: Prevalence of failure to thrive

Author and location of study	Definition	Prevalence of FTT
Batchelor *et al*, 1996 Two districts in southern England	FTT= 1) children under three years whose rate of growth had dropped for three consecutive months from a previously established centile, crossing major centile lines 2) those who had fallen below the 3rd centile for weight	3.9%
Corbett *et al*, 1996 Deprived area of Newcastle (same as Edwards *et al*, 1990)	FTT= children aged <18 months with lowest 3% of thrive index* values who were born at or above 37 weeks gestation and who had no organic condition	13.2%
Skuse *et al*, 1994 London	FTT = children with weight for age index <-1.8 z scores at 12 months of age and sustained for three months. Pre-term, severe intrauterine growth retarded babies and multiple births excluded.	3.3%
Edwards *et al*, 1990 Deprived area of Newcastle	FTT= a child whose weight deviates during the first two years of life downwards across two or more major centiles from the maximum centile achieved at 4-8 weeks for a period of a month or more	20.9%

*The Thrive index is a standard for weight gain in infancy which quantified the normal variation in weight gain as well as adjusting for regression to the mean.

5.5.3.ii *The role of nutrition*

Approximately 5% of cases of slow weight gain during infancy can be attributed to disease (gastro-intestinal, endocrine, or other chronic disease) (Skuse *et al*, 1994; Wright & Talbot, 1996; Corbett *et al*, 1996). The remainder can be attributed to psycho-social causes in which undernutrition forms a final common pathway (Skuse *et al*, 1994; Raynor *et al*, 1996). Dietary assessment and the estimation of energy requirements in children suffering from FTT is fraught with methodological problems as body composition and diet may both have changed by the time the condition is apparent (Wright *et al,* 2000).

In a retrospective study Wright *et al* (1996) noted that 50% of a sample of FTT children had already met FTT criteria by 6 months. Most of those remaining had faltered in weight gain before this age. This demonstrates that early infant feeding patterns are a critical aspect of pathogenesis. In a sample of FTT children multiple regression analysis showed that weight at 4 weeks, 6 weeks and 3 months was very significantly positively associated with exclusive breastfeeding. Breastfeeding was not therefore a factor contributing to FTT. In contrast, sleeping through feeds was consistently negatively associated with weight (Skuse *et al,* 1994). Later introduction of solids and poor dietary variety have also been associated with FTT, though may be consequences rather than causes (Wright *et al,* 2000).

The reasons children receive insufficient food are unclear and not always amenable to simple dietary advice (Wright *et al,* 1996). Even in affluent circumstances children may fail to thrive as the result of inadequate parenting, problems with the child's temperament and appetite, parental psychopathology, poor parent-child interaction or family dysfunction (Raynor *et al,* 1996). Well-designed studies supporting these associations are however rare (Boddy & Skuse 1994; Skuse *et al,* 1994).

5.5.3.iii *The consequences of FTT*
The long term consequences of FTT on cognitive development have been most frequently researched. In a small study of children who were chronically underweight throughout their pre-school years 35% had General Cognitive Index (GCI) scores below 70 points and were likely to require special educational provision upon entry into school (Dowdney *et al,* 1987). Such dramatic consequences have not been demonstrated by others and reverse causation[1] is difficult to exclude. Follow-up at age 7-9 years of a cohort who failed to thrive in infancy showed that cases were significantly shorter than controls: after adjusting for parental heights a difference of 4.4cm remained. Case children were also significantly lighter and had lower body mass index (BMI) and head circumference. There were no significant differences in cognitive attainment (Drewett *et al,* 1999).

5.5.3.iv *Who is at risk?*
FTT seems to be one result of a "malevolent combination of benign and subtle factors linked to child rearing". They are more prevalent in deprived circumstances though deprivation itself cannot clearly be identified as a cause (Wright, 1999, personal communication). In Newcastle, twice as many children living in deprived areas were classified as failing to thrive (defined by "Thrive Index" <1.48) as those living in intermediate areas. However, children in affluent

---

[1] Reverse causation means that the outcome being measured may be the cause rather than the consequence of the association observed.

households were also significantly more likely than children in intermediate households to fall below the Thrive Index threshold. Nearly half the deficit between affluent and deprived children at 1 year of age was attributable to variation in post-natal growth rather than birth weight (Wright *et al*, 1994b).

5.5.3.v   *Conclusions*

- The process leading to "failure-to-thrive" (FTT) begins in early infancy when growth velocity is greatest.

- FTT has major consequences for overall growth though influences of cognitive development have been less clearly demonstrated.

- Undernutrition forms the final common pathway to FTT beneath which a host of social, economic, educational and psychological factors operate. In the context of this country it seems unlikely that FTT could be prevented or treated through provision of food or simple dietary advice alone.

- Although FTT is commoner in areas of deprivation it is possible that the existing provisions of the Welfare Food Scheme mask a clear causative link to food shortage.

5.5.4   Catch-up of Low Birth Weight

Low birth weight infants, particularly those born prematurely, see section 5.4.1.i) are nutritionally disadvantaged compared with those of normal birth weight (DHSS, 1988) for a number of reasons:

- They have reduced body stores at birth

- Rates of *potential* postnatal growth are high, imposing demands for energy and other nutrients

- Physiological systems are immature, compromising maintenance of homeostasis

- Severe morbidity, particularly affecting the cardiorespiratory system, is common. This may influence both tolerance of food and utilisation of nutrients for growth.

The smaller and more immature the baby, the greater the nutritional risk. Breastfeeding is considered the safest option but a range of nutrient-enriched formulas and supplements is available for use on prescription under dietetic and medical supervision, both within hospital and after discharge home. The majority of Low Birth Weight infants, particularly those born pre-term, move towards patterns of infant feeding similar to normal infants as they catch up in weight for age (Department of Health, 1994). COMA recommended that weaning should begin when the infant weighs at least 5kg, has lost the extrusion reflex and is able to eat from a spoon. Fussy eaters and those difficult to feed may require special attention to ensure that the diet remains adequate (Department of Health, 1994). Later iron deficiency is commoner amongst infants of low birthweight (*vide infra*), reflecting their lower iron stores at birth. Early medicinal iron supplementation is recommended

Low birthweight is likely to occur more commonly in families eligible for WFS benefits (section 5.4.1.iv). Important foods provided by the Scheme in this context are vitamins (particularly C and D) and infant formula for those not breastfed. An anomaly of the current provisions is that entitlement to formula ceases at 1 year of *chronological* age without adjustment for prematurity. In effect this results in earlier loss of entitlement for the babies most at risk. For example, the entitlement of an infant born at 24-28 weeks of gestation would cease at 8-9 months of corrected age rather than 1 year. Introduction of liquid cow's milk to such an infant would be particularly undesirable as risk of iron deficiency would be increased (section 5.6.1.iv). There is a strong case for continuing entitlement to formula until 1 year from the *expected date of confinement* rather than the date of birth, and perhaps even further beyond.

5.6   Young children

5.6.1   Anaemia and iron deficiency

5.6.1.i   *Prevalence*
Table 5.8 indicates that the reported prevalence of anaemia varies markedly between populations studied. The definition used, age at testing (James *et al*, 1995), and prevalence of haemoglobinopathies and other medical conditions all strongly influence this quantity. The NDNS showed that more than one in ten children aged 1½-2½ years were anaemic (haemoglobin concentrations <11.0g /dl). This fell to 6% for children aged 2½-3½ years and further as boys grew

Table 5.8: Prevalence of anaemia in young children

Author	Subjects		Criteria used	Prevalence
Gregory *et al* 1995 Nationally representative (Great Britain)	18-29 months		Hb <11.0 g/l Ferritin <10µg/l	12% 28%
	30-41 months		Hb <11.0g/l Ferritin <10µg/l	6% 18%
Lawson *et al*, 1998 Nationally representative sample of Asian children	24 months	Bangladeshi	Hb <11.0 g/l Ferritin <10µg/l	25% 39%
		Pakistani	Hb <11.0g/l Ferritin <10µg/l	29% 45%
		Indian	Hb <11.0g/l Ferritin <10µg/l	20% 41%
Emond *et al* 1996 Bristol (ALSPAC study)	8 months		Hb <11.0g/l	23%
James *et al*, 1997 5 practices in Bristol	13-14 months		Hb <11.0g/l	0-35%
Childs *et al*, 1997 Inner city Birmingham	18 months		Hb <11.0g/l	27%
Sherriff *et al*, 1999 (ALSPAC study)	12 months		Hb <110g/l Ferritin <10µg/l	18% 0.4%
	18 months		Hb <11.0g/l Ferritin <10µg/l	17.3% 2.5%

older, but remained at 8% for 3½-4½ year old girls (Gregory *et al*, 1995). Prevalence in a nationally representative sample of Asian children was considerably higher than the NDNS sample (Lawson *et al*, 1998).

5.6.1.ii *Consequences of iron deficiency anaemia*

The functional consequences of iron deficiency anaemia have been long recognised. Non-haematological effects include disturbance of muscle and gastrointestinal function, susceptibility to infection, poor growth and behavioural disturbance. The consequences for neurological development have not yet been clearly established; although most studies can be methodologically flawed, evidence in general points to some effect (Logan, 1999). Inconsistency of evidence from supplementation studies (using iron-fortified formula or medicinal iron) is partly due to the limitations of development scales (de Andraca *et al*, 1997; Lansdown & Wharton, 1995); additional dietary iron may more strongly affect some developmental fields more than others. The age of onset, severity and duration of anaemia may also be important. Findings of secondary prevention studies may therefore differ from those focused on primary prevention (see Table 5.9).

Table 5.9: Key studies examining the impact of iron on cognitive development

Study details	Period of intervention	Iron delivered	Impact on cognitive development
PRIMARY PREVENTION			
Moffat *et al*, 1994 Canada	0-2 months-15 months	"Low-iron" formula (0.1mg/100ml) cf "Iron fortified" formula (1.3mg/100ml)	Significantly better psychomotor development scores (Bayley) at 9 and 12 months but not at 15 months
Morley *et al*, 1999 3 centres in UK	9-18 months	Cow's milk Infant formula cf (0.9mg/100ml) Follow-on formula (1.2mg / 100ml)	No significant differences between groups using Bayley scores
Williams *et al*, 1999 Birmingham	7-18 months	Cow's milk cf Follow-on formula (1.2mg/100ml)	Significant reduction in decline in Griffiths general quotient scores among formula group at 24 months
SECONDARY PREVENTION			
Idjradinata & Pollitt, 1993 Indonesia	4 months for children aged 12-18 months	Placebo cf 3mg /kg body weight per day	Development delays (Bayley) were reversed in treatment group. No effects were noted in non-anaemic iron deficient and iron sufficient samples
Aukett *et al*, 1986 Birmingham	2 months for children aged 17-19 months	10mg vitamin C cf 24 mg iron and 10mg vitamin C	Significantly more treated children achieved the expected rate of development (Denver development screening test)

Amongst secondary prevention studies, an Indonesian randomised double blind, placebo controlled trial which recruited anaemic children aged 12-18 months showed a pronounced rise in Bayley mental and motor scores following iron supplementation (Idjradinata & Pollitt, 1993) but no effect was noted among non-anaemic iron deficient or iron-sufficient groups. A previous study in the UK (Aukett *et al*, 1986) showed an increase in development skills in the treated group.

Two recent UK primary prevention studies have measured the effect of iron-fortified formula on mental and psychomotor development (Williams *et al*, 1999; Morley *et al*, 1999). The first randomly allocated a group of 6-month old children of low socio-economic status to receive iron fortified follow-on formula (1.2 mg/100ml) or cow's milk for one year. There was no difference between the groups in the development score at 18 months but a significant difference in the prevalence of anaemia. (2% of infants receiving formula versus 33% of those on cow's milk). At 2 years the Griffiths general quotient score had declined in both groups and significantly more in those receiving cow's milk ($p<0.02$). The authors noted that personal and social skills were positively affected by supplementation. They suggested that poor performance in these areas might underlie impairment of learning skills in iron deficient children (Williams *et al* 1999). Morley *et al* (1999) compared children fed high or low iron-fortified formula (0.9mg/100ml and 1.2mg/100ml) or cow's milk from ages 9-18 months. There were no significant differences between groups in Bayley psychomotor or mental development scores at 18 months but this might reflect the relatively early age of testing. Moreover, the haematological data were incomplete and few infants from "high risk" groups appear to have been included. Williams *et al* (1999) also failed to detect differences at 18 months study though an effect became apparent later (*vide supra*). A Canadian study noted a transient effect of iron fortified formula (1.3mg/100ml) compared to low iron formula (0.1mg/100ml) on developmental attainment at 9-12 months of age (Moffat *et al*, 1994).

Two-months of medicinal iron supplementation given to anaemic children aged 17-19 months promoted weight gain in a UK study (Aukett *et al*, 1986). In another study supplementation of iron-replete children had a negative effect on weight gain (Idjradinata *et al*, 1994).

5.6.1.iii *The role of nutrition*
Milk intake is the dietary variable most consistently associated with iron status, though it explains only a small part of the overall variance in measures examined (Lawson *et al*, 1998). Early introduction of liquid cow's milk has been associated with a significantly increased incidence of anaemia (Mills, 1990; Booth & Aukett, 1997; Lawson *et al*, 1998). Table 5.10 shows the proportion of children who received cow's milk by country and age in the UK.

Table 5.10: Percentage of mothers giving cow's milk as the main milk by country and age (Foster *et al*, 1997)

	England and Wales	Scotland	Northern Ireland
% mothers who gave cows milk as the main milk to babies aged 8-9 months	14	20	23
	6 weeks	5 months	9 months
% mothers who gave cow's milk in United Kingdom	0	1	13

Table 5.11 shows the key findings from randomised primary prevention studies examining the effect of different types of milk on the iron status of infants and young children.

• Daly *et al* (1996) studied replacement of cow's milk with iron fortified formula (1.2mg/100ml) between 6 and 18 months in a deprived area of Birmingham. No children receiving formula were anaemic at 2 years, compared to 26% of those who remained on cow's milk (Daly *et al*, 1996).

• Gill *et al* (1997) showed that low iron formula (0.1mg/100ml) improved iron status when compared to cow's milk, though a slightly greater effect was noted in the high iron formula (1.3mg/100ml) group.

• Moffat *et al* (1994) reported benefits in infancy associated with a formula containing 1.3 mg/100 ml as opposed to 0.1 mg/100ml.

• In contrast to the findings of Moffatt *et al* (1994) and Gill *et al* (1997), a study in Gloucester showed that iron-fortified formula (1.2mg per 100ml) was no more effective than unfortified formula (0.1mg per 100ml) in preventing anaemia (Stevens & Nelson, 1995).

Table 5.11: Effects of cow's milk and fortified formula milk on iron status: key studies

Study details	Period of intervention	Iron content of milk in different groups	Impact on anaemia
Daly *et al*, 1996, Birmingham	6-18 months	Cow's milk cf Follow-on formula (1.2mg/100ml)	Significant prevention of anaemia in formula group
Gill *et al*, 1997 21 centres in UK and Ireland	6-15 months	Cow's milk cf Follow-on formula (1.2mg/100ml) Low iron formula (0.14mg/100ml)	Significantly different Hb concentrations between groups (cow's milk lowest and high iron formula highest) at 15 months
Stevens *et al*, 1995 Gloucester	6-18 months	Low-iron formula (0.1mg/100ml) cf Follow-on formula (1.2mg/100ml)	No difference between groups in serum ferritin and haemoglobin concentration
Moffat *et al*, 1994 Canada	0-2 months-15 months	"Low iron" formula (0.1mg/100ml) cf "Iron fortified" formula (1.3mg/100ml)	Significantly higher haematological indices among higher iron formula group at all stages

None of these studies included either a breastfed reference group or one fed a standard UK infant formula (iron content about 0.6mg/100ml). The most marked differences were those observed between infants fed liquid cow's milk and formula, whatever its iron content. This has been attributed to cow's milk provoking occult blood loss (Daly *et al*, 1996) or inhibiting iron absorption due to the other nutrients present (Department of Health, 1994). It has therefore not been shown directly that a follow-on formula containing >1mg/100ml of iron has any advantage over standard formula (as opposed to liquid cow's milk) in maintaining iron status.

Although non-milk dietary sources of iron are less strongly correlated with iron status (Grindulis *et al*, 1986; Warrington & Storey, 1989; (James *et al*, 1995;

Childs *et al*, 1997; Lawson *et al*, 1998), the NDNS showed a positive relationship between total dietary intake of haem and non-haem iron and haemoglobin status (Gregory *et al*, 1995). The generally weak relationships have been explained by the difficulty of accurately measuring iron intake in this age group and the confounding presence of enhancers or inhibitors of iron absorption. It may also be confounded by the negative relationship between rapid weight gain and iron status (Emond *et al*, 1996) (section 5.6.1.iv). Children aged 18-30 months are most likely to have intakes below DRV (Payne & Belton, 1992; Gregory *et al*, 1995) (Table 23). NDNS showed that 24% of children in this age group had dietary iron intakes below the LRNI.

Table 5.12: Mean daily intakes of iron among young children

	6-12 months (Mills & Tyler, 1992)	18-30 months (Gregory *et al*, 1995)	30-42 months (Gregory *et al*, 1995)
RNI (mg/day)	7.8	6.9	6.9
Mean Intake (mg/day)	8.1	5.0	5.6

5.6.1.iv *Who is at risk?*

Iron deficiency anaemia is more common among certain ethnic groups (Ehrhardt, 1986; D'Souza *et al*, 1987; Warrington & Storey, 1989; Lawson *et al*, 1998) (see Table 19). A study in inner city Birmingham of children aged 18 months showed that 19% of those with white European background were anaemic whereas 27% of those with Asian background and 29% of those with Afro-Caribbean background were affected (Childs *et al*, 1997). Table 5.13 indicates that Asian babies are more likely than white ones to be given cow's milk before 15 months. Milk intakes of Asian children are also higher than those of white children (Mills, 1990), perhaps indicating reduced exposure to other dietary iron sources. Higher phytate and fibre intakes in the diets of Asian children may impair uptake of iron, particularly in ethnic minority groups who are vegetarian. A lack of commercially available Halal complementary foods may also constrain meat intake (D'Souza *et al*,1987; Warrington & Storey, 1989) (section 5.8.4.iii).

Table 5.13: Percentage of babies receiving cow's milk as their main source of milk by age and ethnicity (Thomas & Avery, 1997)

	Bangladeshi	Pakistani	Indian	White
5 months*	1	4	3	1
9 months	27	30	23	20**
15 months	86	86	85	79

* not necessarily as a main drink
** this is considerably higher than in the Infant Feeding Survey 1995 (Table 21, page 64)

The early introduction of cow's milk has been independently associated with low maternal age and educational attainment in a study of 8-month old children living in South West England (North *et al*, 2000). Fourteen per cent of this sample were receiving neither breastmilk nor formula at the age of 8 months. A higher number of older siblings, and difficulty in affording food were also significant risk factors (North *et al*, 2000).

Three studies based on national samples have failed to demonstrate a relationship between anaemia in young children and the social class or educational attainment of the mother (Gregory *et al*, 1995; Lawson *et al*, 1998; Emond *et al*, 1996). Grindulis *et al* (1986) however showed that mother's educational status and father's social class were related to the proportion of children whose haemoglobin concentration was under 10 g/dl. Sherrif *et al* (1999) demonstrated a "U"-shaped relationship between maternal educational attainment and haemoglobin status at 18 months. Prevalence was greatest among children whose mothers had a university degree and lowest amongst those whose mothers had a vocational qualification. The authors suggested this might have been a statistical anomaly.

Weight gain has been shown to be negatively associated with iron status (Sherrif *et al*, 1999; Lawson *et al*, 1998; Emond *et al*, 1996). This may reflect rapid weight gain among low birth weight babies showing catch-up growth. Such children may also have lower iron stores at birth and be at particular risk of iron deficiency.

Dietary intakes of both iron and vitamin C (which enhances the absorption of non-haem iron) were both shown to be independently related to socio-economic factors in the NDNS survey (Gregory *et al*, 1995). Lower intakes of both were associated with manual social class. Lower vitamin C intake was also associated with receipt of benefits. Indeed plasma vitamin C concentrations showed marked variations with socio-economic indicators (Gregory *et al*, 1995).

5.6.1.v   *Conclusions*

- Iron deficiency anaemia is widespread among pre-school children in the UK and is likely to have negative effects on mental and motor development.

- Those from ethnic minority (particularly Asian) backgrounds are at greater risk.

- Early introduction of cow's milk is strongly associated with later development of anaemia.

- There is some evidence that continuing to use infant formula rather than liquid cow's milk into the second year of life reduces the prevalence of anaemia and supports better neurological development.

- A number of other factors have been independently associated with the development of iron deficiency. These include low birthweight, prolonged dependence on cow's milk at the expense of a more varied diet, and low vitamin C intake. Although each is associated with low socio-economic status, evidence of a direct relationship between iron deficiency and parental educational attainment or social class is inconsistent.

5.6.2   Vitamin D deficiency

5.6.2.i   *Prevalence*

The NDNS of children 1½ to 4½ years old indicated that 1% of children aged 1½-4½ years had plasma 25-hydroxyvitamin D levels <25 nmol/l, a value generally taken to indicate deficiency. There were no apparent associations between 25-hydroxyvitamin D levels and the age or sex of children. Despite the rarity of deficiency in the population studied, intakes of those aged 1½-3 years averaged approximately a quarter of the RNI. This confirms the important contribution adequate sunlight exposure must make to vitamin D status.

5.6.2.ii   *Who is at risk?*

The NDNS data mask considerable variation between different groups of the population. Plasma 25-hydroxyvitamin D levels of a nationally representative sample of Asian children aged 2 years were strikingly lower than those of white controls matched for age and place of residence. Twenty per cent of Bangladeshi, 34% of Pakistani and 25% of Indian children had plasma levels below 25 nmol/l (Lawson *et al*, 1999a).   Thirteen to eighteen per cent of children had concentrations <20nmol/l, a level typically associated with rickets (Department of Health, 1998b). Blood samples in this study (the "Asian Feeding Survey") were taken in the months of October and November. Amongst children in the NDNS sample studied at a comparable time of year only 1% fell below 25nmol/l (Gregory *et al*, 1995).

Multiple regression analysis of the "Asian Feeding Survey" data have confirmed diet to be an important component of aetiology. For all Asian children the concentration of plasma vitamin D was positively associated with consumption of vitamin supplements. Use of infant formula at 15 months of age was also a significant predictor among Indian and Pakistani children. Bivariate analysis showed consumption of chapati at 15 months to be a significant independent variable associated with low plasma concentrations in Indian and Pakistani children (Lawson *et al*, 1999b). Indian children, living in the north of England showed significantly lower vitamin D levels than those living in the south. Indicators of iron deficiency – low haemoglobin and serum ferritin concentrations – were consistently associated with low plasma 25-hydroxyvitamin D concentrations. Other studies have also noted this association (Grindulis *et al*, 1986; Wharton, 1999).

Although it is recognised that most children meet their vitamin D requirements from normal diet and exposure to sunlight, the recommendations for supplementation (sections 4.6.1.ii and 4.7.1) form a "safety net" for vulnerable groups and individuals (for example: those prone to periods of low dietary intake, those whose bodies are completely covered by clothing or potent sunscreen (Zlotkin, 1999) when out of doors, and children born to women who were vitamin D deficient during pregnancy).

Compared to white infants, significantly more Asian infants receive supplements (Thomas & Avery, 1997). Although there are no national data about Afro-

Caribbean children, a study of primary school children showed that they too were more likely to receive supplements than white children, and that cod liver oil supplements were used by a quarter (Bristow *et al*, 1997). In keeping with social class effects noted in the 1995 Infant Feeding Survey, the NDNS 1½ to 4½ years showed that supplement consumption was significantly higher among non-manual (27%) than manual social classes (13%) and increased with the age of the child (Table 5.14) (Gregory *et al*, 1995). Approximately half of the supplements consumed by children in the NDNS sample contained vitamin D (NDNS 1½-4½ years, unpublished data).

Table 5.14: Dietary supplement use by infants and young children

Recipient of supplement	% General population (Foster *et al*, 1997 and Gregory *et al*, 1995)	% Bangladeshi	% Pakistani	% Indian	% White
		(Thomas & Avery, 1997)			
Infants aged 6-10 weeks	6[1]	15	22	21	7
Infants aged 4-5 months	10[1]	32	41	39	9
Infants aged 8-9 months	27[1]	52	57	56	20
Infants aged 8-9 months	25[2]				
Children aged 1½-2½ yrs	17	43*	38*	46*	NA
Children aged 2½-3½ yrs	19	NA	NA	NA	NA
Children aged 3½-4½ yrs	22	NA	NA	NA	NA

* aged two years (Lawson *et al*, 1998)   NA = not available
[1] breastfed babies only, 2 babies fed cow's milk as their main milk

5.6.2.iii *Conclusions*

- Plasma 25-hydroxyvitamin D levels identify children from Asian ethnic backgrounds as the group most at risk of vitamin D deficiency.

- There are no comparable, national data for children of Afro-Caribbean background.

- Low plasma vitamin D concentrations are infrequently encountered in other population groups despite low dietary intake and poor compliance with recommendations about the use of vitamin D supplements.

- Nutritional factors relevant to aetiology of vitamin D deficiency in children of Asian background include the use of chapatis and low uptake of vitamin supplements. Although as a group they are more likely to take supplements than white children and women, over a half still take nothing.

- Iron deficiency and vitamin D deficiency are likely to co-exist amongst Asian children. It is noteworthy in this context that continued consumption of infant formula beyond 1 year of age not only reduces the risk of iron deficiency (section 6.6.1.iii) but is a predictor of plasma 25-hydroxyvitamin D concentration.

- National data suggest that those in lower social class groups are least likely to take dietary supplements though it is not known whether this applies in ethnic groups most at risk.

5.6.3   Dental caries

5.6.3.i   *Prevalence*
The National Diet and Nutrition Survey of children aged 1½-4½ years included a dental survey. The prevalence of dental caries was higher among older children and almost one in three children aged 3½-4½ years had some degree of decay (Table 5.15). Only 30 of the 208 health districts in the United Kingdom were classified as having fluoridated water in 1997 (British Fluoridation Society, 1997).

Table 5.15: Percentage of dental decay among children aged 1½-4½ years exhibiting decay (Hinds *et al*, 1995)

Type of decay (%)	Age of child (years)			
	1½-2½	2½-3½	3½- 4½	All ages
Active decay	4	13	28	16
Filled teeth	-	1	4	2
Teeth missing due to decay	0	1	4	2
Any decay	4	14	30	17

5.6.3.ii   *Who is at risk?*
Children in Wales, Scotland and the north of England showed more decayed teeth than those in other parts of England. The prevalence of any decay experience was between 6% and 18% higher among children whose parents were in receipt of benefit, the proportion rising with age. This marked disparity between households of high and low socio-economic status has also been noted in a number of local studies (e.g. Provart & Carmichael, 1995; Ellwood & O'Mullane, 1996; Tickle *et al*, 1999; Jones & Worthington, 1999). Measures of household socio-economic status seem stronger predictors of caries prevalence than either dietary factors or dental care (seeing a dentist or brushing teeth).

There is no consistent evidence that infants fed a cow's milk protein-based formula are at greater risk of caries than those breastfed. Soya formulas, however, contain non-milk sugars (glucose polymers) which are more cariogenic than lactose. As only 3% of infants are fed using soya formula (Foster *et al*, 1997) the number potentially affected would appear to be small. Fluoridation of the public water supply has greatest potential for reducing the incidence of caries in young children receiving formula as compliance with medicinal fluoride supplements appears to be poor and cannot be universally applied (section 4.7.1)

In the NDNS 1½-4½ years, multi-variate analysis of the factors independently related to dental decay showed that receipt of IS or FC were significantly and independently associated with tooth decay among children aged 1½-2½ years.

Among those 2½-3½ years of age the mother's highest educational qualification and consumption of sugary drinks in bed were the significant predictor variables. Social class, region of residence, household spending on confectionery and receipt of benefit were all significant independent variables amongst the oldest group. After stepwise logistic regression the strength of the association between social class and caries rate was twice that of the association between tooth-brushing and caries, and nearly three times that between sugar confectionery consumption and caries. This suggests that socio-economic factors outweigh dietary factors in importance.

Although dietary patterns differed, total average intakes of non-milk extrinsic (NME) sugars were not significantly different between children from manual and non-manual classes. Children from manual classes were more likely to have been fed from a bottle, to have had confectionery and carbonated drinks more frequently, to have come from households which spend more money on confectionery each week, and to have consumed more table sugar (often in tea or coffee). In contrast, those from non-manual households were more likely to have drunk fruit juice (which overall contributed 39% of NME sugars), sugars, preserves and confectionery (contributing 27%) and were more likely to have received a drink in bed (Hinds & Gregory, 1995; Gregory *et al*, 1995).

In general, the risk associated with consumption of sugars seems more strongly related to the *frequency* of consumption than the overall quantity. Although NDNS did not record the frequency of consumption, a study of two communities with differing prevalence of caries in North West England showed that the median frequency of NME sugar consumption episodes[18] was 10.5 in the high-caries community compared to 6 in the low-caries community. The difference was accounted for largely by consumption of sugary drinks to which more children in the high caries community had unrestricted access, even when out of the house (Jones & Hussey, 1996). Although the "high-caries" community was of lower overall socio-economic status the study did not attempt to establish a relationship between social class and frequency of consumption. Another study reached similar overall conclusions but also failed to confirm such a relationship (Holt, 1991).

Water fluoridation has been shown to prevent dental caries to a greater extent among deprived communities. It has been estimated that water fluoridation is associated with a 43% reduction in the mean number of decayed, missing or filled primary teeth in wards with a Townsend Score at the national average (Jones & Worthington, 1999) (Figure 5.3). While fluoridation ameliorates the effect of social deprivation on tooth decay, it does not eradicate the socio-economic gradient (Provart & Carmichael, 1995; Riley *et al*, 1999; Jones & Worthington, 1999) (Figure 5.3).

Figure 5.3: The mean dmft[1] and Townsend Score by non, artificially and naturally fluoridated wards with best fit regression line[2]

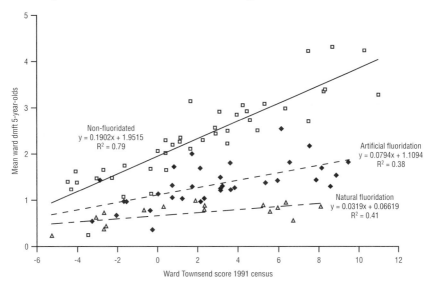

[1] decayed, filled or missing primary teeth
[2] reproduced with kind permission from the authors and with agreement from the British Dental Journal

5.6.3.iii *Conclusions*

- Social class, receipt of benefit and parental educational attainment most strongly predict the development of caries.

- Important dietary factors include frequent consumption of sugary drinks (particularly from a bottle) and the use of soya formula.

- Fluoridation has an important role in preventing dental caries, particularly in deprived communities.

5.6.4   Diarrhoea and fruit juice consumption

Children can regulate their dietary energy intake to varying degrees by compensating with a higher or lower intake than that of a previous meal (Shea *et al*, 1990). Drinking large quantities of energy-rich fluids, such as sweetened soft drinks and fruit squashes, may therefore suppress appetite at mealtimes. It has been suggested that this may affect growth though a recent study of excessive consumption of fruit juice among children aged 2-3 years showed no effect (Skinner *et al*, 1999). High fluid intake and malabsorption of the carbohydrate and saccharide present in fruit drinks and squashes may also cause loose stools (Green & Grishan, 1983). It has been postulated that this may be a cause of chronic non-specific diarrhoea in young children (or "toddlers' diarrhoea") (Lifshitz & Ament, 1992; Treem, 1992). In 1991, the American Academy of Pediatrics drew attention to the problems encountered in children who ingest excessive amounts of fruit juice. It recommended that a dietary history be obtained for any child presenting with chronic diarrhoea, abdominal pain or bloating (AAP, 1991).

Many drinks given to pre-school children in the UK are based on fruit products and have a high energy content. Data from ALSPAC on 4 and 8 month old infants showed that 17% of mothers gave fruit juice and 56% gave squash or cordial to their babies (Emmet *et al*, 2000). A small study in Southampton suggested that about 15% of 2-7 year olds obtained around 50% of their daily energy requirements from such drinks (Hourihane *et al*, 1995). The NDNS provided some data on variation in soft drink consumption with social class in Great Britain. Intake was higher among the manual social classes but data are not available on the incidence of toddlers' diarrhoea.

5.7   Schoolchild and adolescent

5.7.1   Fatness
In adults the term obesity is defined operationally in terms of association with adverse health outcomes. There are no equivalent associations for weight in relation to height during childhood, therefore some care needs to be exercised with terminology. Although BMI charts have recently become available (section 5.2.3) there is little experience of their use in clinical practice. If the term obesity is to be used, then there is the need to be explicit about how it has been defined, and some justification for that definition.

5.7.1.i   *Prevalence*
Successive generations of children in England and Scotland are becoming fatter (Hughes *et al*, 1997). The 1996 Health Survey for England estimated that 4% of children aged 2-15 years were obese using a definition based on a Body Mass Index (BMI) above the 1990 UK reference 98th percentile (Prescott-Clarke & Primatesta, 1998).

5.7.1.ii   *Health consequences of fatness*
Rona *et al* (1996) showed that heavier or fatter 9 year old children had higher systolic and diastolic blood pressures and cholesterol concentrations after controlling for other confounders.

The long-term mortality and morbidity risks associated with obesity in childhood are not well understood (Power *et al*, 1997a), though associations between adult obesity and adverse health outcomes such as cardiovascular disease, non-insulin dependent diabetes, hypertension and some forms of cancer are well established (Serdula *et al*, 1993). Adolescent overweight has been associated with coronary heart disease, atherosclerosis and colorectal cancer mortality in males and arthritis and functional limitation in women (Power *et al*, 1997a). The socio-economic risks of obesity especially among young women have also been highlighted in a US population (Gortmaker *et al*, 1993).

There is some evidence that fat children have a higher risk of becoming obese adults, though the strength of the relationship varies between studies (Parsons *et al*, 1999). Analysis of the 1958 British birth cohort showed that 9% of obese 33 year old women had been overweight at the age of 7 years (Power *et al*, 1997a). The excess risk of fat children remaining obese into adulthood has been shown to be 2 to 6.5 fold and was greatest among those who were older and fatter (Serdula *et al*, 1993). Those children who remained overweight in adulthood were also likely to have experienced earlier puberty (Power *et al*, 1997b). Evidence of the tracking of lifestyle factors such as diet and physical exercise from child to adulthood provides further justification for identifying children at risk of obesity (Parsons *et al*, 1999).

5.7.1.iii *The role of nutrition*
The influence of early childhood dietary practices on weight in later life has been examined in a small number of longitudinal studies recently reviewed (Parsons *et al*, 1999). Positive associations between protein intake at 2 years of age and BMI at 8 years have been noted (Rolland-Cachera *et al*, 1995) though findings overall are inconsistent. It has been suggested that the relationship between fatness and diet may be most evident when acting in combination with other lifestyle factors (Parsons *et al*, 1999).

There is a paucity of data on the contribution of school children's diets to obesity, a problem compounded by the difficulty of assessing intake accurately and systematic under-reporting by obese subjects (Summerbell *et al*, 1996). Reduced energy requirements due to decline in physical activity may be as important as dietary factors (Prentice & Jebb, 1995), so the recently noted decline in the physical activity of school age children is of concern. In a cross-sectional study the sum of skinfold thickness measurements was one of three social and biological factors independently associated with physical fitness (Kikuchi *et al*, 1995) though the direction of causation cannot be confirmed .

5.7.1.iv *Who is at risk?*
Analysis of data from the National Study of Health and Growth of primary school children (a longitudinal study including several samples) collected between 1972 and 1994 identified vulnerable groups (Chinn, 1995). Increases in triceps skinfold thickness measurements were greater in Scotland than England and greatest among Scottish girls who had the highest skinfold thickness at the end of the study. Ethnicity also has an effect: Punjabi and Urdu boys had significantly higher mean skinfold thickness measurements than a representative white sample (Rona & Chinn, 1997).

Multiple regression analysis of the social and biological factors associated with childhood measurements of skinfold thickness showed that biological factors outweighed social influences (Duran-Tauleria *et al*, 1995), birthweight and parental BMI being most important. Analysis of child overweight as a binary variable in multiple logistic regression further indicated that children whose mothers worked for fewer than 15 hours a week outside the home, and children from large families were less likely to be overweight. Children at greatest risk came from families with a single parent (particularly if the parent was male), or those in which the father was in skilled manual occupation (Duran-Tauleria *et al*, 1995). These models explained less than 15% of the variation in child fatness however. This further emphasises the problem of identifying children vulnerable to the development of obesity and its consequences.

The Health Survey for England indicated no consistent relationship between overall activity level and social class. Children from lower social classes were less likely to participate in sport but more likely to walk regularly and take part in active play (especially older boys). Girls were more likely to do gardening or housework than children in higher social classes (Prescott-Clark & Primatesta, 1998).

5.7.1.v *Conclusions*

• The prevalence of childhood fatness is increasing in the UK.

• Fat children face at least a two-fold greater risk of becoming obese as adults. This poses significant risk to long-term health.

• The relative contributions made by diet and physical exercise to the development of childhood fatness are poorly quantified.

• Social factors seem less important contributors to the development of fatness than birthweight and parental body mass index.

5.7.2   Dietary patterns of schoolchildren

Older schoolgirls are at greatest risk of having nutrient intakes which fall short of DRVs (section 4.8.2). Minerals (particularly iron, magnesium, zinc and calcium) are most likely to be consumed in low quantities. Supplementation with milk has been reviewed in section 6.4.3. Boys' intakes of energy and most micronutrients were lower in households receiving benefit though there were few differences for girls. After adjustment for energy intake, few significant differences remained (NDNS 4-18 years unpublished data).

Table 5.16 shows data from NDNS 4-18 years on the proportion of children who "skipped" breakfast over a 7 day period. Skipping breakfast was more common amongst children from households in receipt of benefit though it did not reach statistical significance for most age groups. As might be expected, a significantly higher proportion of schoolchildren from households receiving benefit ate school meals. For example, half of the 15-18 year olds from benefit households had school meals on most days compared to a quarter from non-benefit households. It has been noted previously that children from low-income families obtain a greater proportion of their nutrient intake from school meals (Nelson & Paul, 1983).

The risks associated with low nutrient intakes during teenage years are most clearly exemplified by conditions such as anorexia and bulimia, which appear to be increasing in prevalence. These may carry risk for reproductive competence (para 5.4.5.i). However, as these are conditions requiring psychological management, we have not considered them further.

Table 5.16: Percentage of children skipping breakfast on school days and in receipt of benefit (Unpublished data from NDNS 4-18 years, Gregory *et al*, 2000)

% of young people skipping breakfast[1] on school days	Age (years)					
	4-10		11-14		15-18	
	Receiving benefits	Not receiving benefits	Receiving benefits	Not receiving benefits	Receiving benefits	Not receiving benefits
% of young people who skip breakfast at least once[2]	20	15	51	36	65	50
Number of young people	34	74	48	107	30	102
% of young people who skip breakfast on most days[3]	6	4	25	16	43	32
Number of young people	10	18	24	48	20	66

[1] breakfast defined as solid food before 9am on school days
[2] young people who skip breakfast on one or more school days during the seven day dietary record
[3] young people who skip breakfast on more than half school days during the seven day record

5.8   Correlates of nutritional vulnerability

The Panel has been asked: *"to characterise any groups particularly vulnerable to nutritional inadequacy, and the vulnerabilities;"*. To date we have identified some adverse nutritional outcomes in the UK population and have characterised the population groups at risk in terms of social class, maternal age, parental educational attainment, ethnicity and measures of income such as receipt of benefit.   We have not, however, explored the mechanisms which link these variables to adverse nutritional outcome. Figures 5.4 and 5.5 highlight the ways in which societal factors, poverty and other factors may influence the child's food consumption and nutritional status.

5.8.1   Social class
We have noted that low social class is associated with the following adverse nutritional outcomes:

- reduced final height (section 5.2.5)

- low birthweight (section 5.4.1.iv)

- low prevalence of breastfeeding (section 5.5.1.ii

- early introduction of solids (section 5.5.2.ii)

- maternal iron deficiency anaemia (section 5.4.2.iv)

- dental caries (section 5.6.3.ii)

Figure 5.4: UNICEF CONCEPTUAL FRAMEWORK: Causes of malnutrition

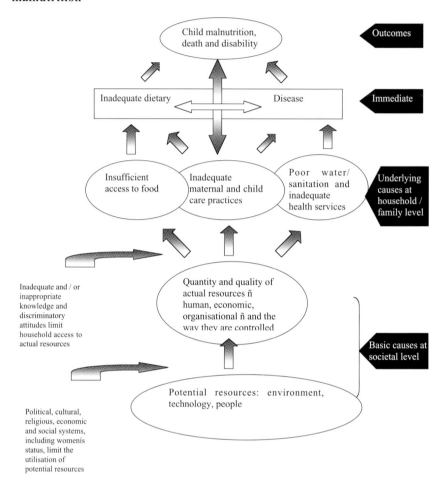

The method of collecting data on social class may affect the classification of pregnant women or young mothers. Much depends on whether occupational information is available:

- whether current or previous occupation is obtained;

- whether a proxy social class is assigned using the occupation from another reference person e.g. husband or partner.

A number of possible mechanisms could be adduced to explain the relationship between low social class and nutritional vulnerability, for example: low income, poor living conditions, and social norms inconsistent with a healthy diet. In subsequent paragraphs we examine evidence for the relative importance of each.

Figure 5.5: Framework of the determinants of food and nutrition security for mothers and their children in the UK

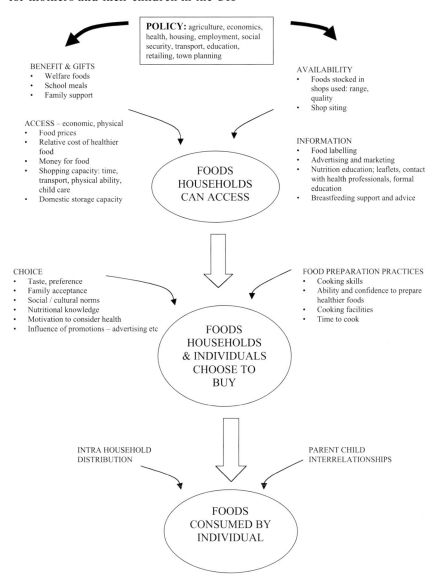

5.8.1.i *The cost of a healthy diet*

Spending on food decreases with lower social class but increases as a proportion of total household expenditure (see Table 28). Households in social class V devoted a fifth of their budget to food in 1997-8 (ONS, 1998a). Analysis of the data according to receipt of benefit indicates that average expenditure on food and drink per person is £5 less for households in receipt of benefit than for those not in receipt of benefit (MAFF, 1998).

Table 5.17: Weekly food expenditure by social class (ONS, 1998a)

	I	II	IIIN	IIIM	IV	V
Average weekly household expenditure (£) on food and non-alcoholic drinks	82.60	71.90	53.00	61.10	50.20	43.50
% of total expenditure spent on food	14.5	15.5	16.9	17.3	19.1	20.4

The cost of a healthy diet has been estimated for different household types by the Family Budget Unit. A *low-cost but acceptable* diet (based on 1998 mainstream supermarket costs in York) described the food purchases necessary to satisfy DRVs for all nutrients, meet guidelines for healthy eating, be palatable and accord with UK consumer preferences. The cost (including alcohol) was estimated to be £59.16 per week for a couple with two children (aged 4 and 10 years) (Parker, 1998). This amount (minus the welfare food and school meal provisions) comprises 31% of the income of such a family in which both parents are out of work and receiving Income Support – a proportion of household expenditure which exceeds that of any social class (Table 5.17). The 1997 National Food Survey showed that food expenditure was less than £59.16 for a household of four for the lowest three income deciles (MAFF, 1998). Other diets, based on a least cost diet analysis and meeting RNI have been constructed by MAFF but would require changes in dietary patterns (Leather, 1996).

This recent analysis by the Family Budget Unit is supported by other studies which conclude that a healthy diet [1] is more expensive (Leather, 1992; Maternity Alliance, 1995). This implies that poverty precludes some households access (NCH, 1991; Dowler & Calvert, 1995; Anderson & Hunt, 1992). Dowler *et al* (1995) showed that dietary quality fell as time elapsed from the day of benefit receipt. Households which were stretching benefits to pay debts were found to have the lowest nutrient intakes (Dowler & Calvert, 1995). Despite this a higher proportion of income is spent on fresh fruit, potatoes and other vegetables in low income households compared to higher income groups (Leather, 1996). In such households fruit and vegetable consumption per person falls as family size increases and in large families is the equivalent of a couple of brussel sprouts and a quarter of an apple per person per day (Leather, 1996). Section 5.6.1.iv described the correlation between children's intakes of vitamin C and socio-economic status.

There is evidence to suggest that parents in low-income families protect their children's diets (NCH, 1991; Dowler & Calvert, 1995; Owens, 1997). Dowler & Calvert (1995) demonstrated that low income was consistently related to indicators of parents' dietary intake but not that of their children. This claim is also supported by NDNS 1½- 4½ years and NDNS 4-18 years. In both studies social class or receipt of benefit was associated with intakes of only a minority of nutrients (Gregory *et al*, 1995, 2000), though there are no recent data on the diets of adults.

---

[1] a varied diet meeting nutritional requirements and consistent with healthy eating patterns.

5.8.1.ii *Access to shops*

Low income households may face reduced physical access to food (Owens, 1997; Leather, 1996; Dowler, 1998). Between 1986 and 1997, the number of superstores in Britain has increased from 457 to 1102 whilst the number of independent shops has fallen by 40% (Policy Action Team 13, 1999). Superstores are frequently located on the outskirts of towns and designed primarily for access by car (Henson, 1992). People on low incomes have less access to a car, find it harder to get to out of town shopping centres and so find it harder to carry and transport food in bulk (Caraher *et al*, 1998). Food prices are on average 24% higher in small local shops compared to supermarkets and discount stores (Piachaud & Webb, 1996). The food choice and quality in local small shops tends to be limited though these shops tend to be used by people on low income (Caraher *et al*, 1998). Rural-urban differences have also been noted: in Scotland food prices are 8% higher in the Highlands and Islands than in Aberdeen (HIE, 1999).

5.8.1.iii *Living conditions*

A recent HEA report on cooking skills found that access to cooking equipment was barely affected by social class or income. Only 1-2% of the sample of 5500 stated their food choice was restricted by cooking facilities (HEA, 1999). Lack of cooking facilities (or sharing of facilities) is most likely to affect homeless families, particularly if they are in temporary accommodation or in homes unfit for habitation (Cade, 1992; Leather, 1992; Power, 1999). One definition of "unfit for habitation" is inadequate food preparation facilities.

In 1997, 108,000 families in England & Wales were registered with Local Authorities as homeless and in need of priority housing; 57% had dependent children and 10% included a pregnant woman (ONS, 1999c). Such households are often placed temporarily in bed and breakfast accommodation, short life housing, private leasing or hostels (Victor, 1997). *Shelter* has reported a further 5000 children in bed and breakfast whose parents were not officially considered homeless. In 1996, 1.47 million homes were classified as "unfit for habitation" though 90% of these were occupied (Shelter Week, 1998).

5.8.1.iv *Socio-cultural environment*

The peer group environment is difficult to define and separate from other factors determining food choice but has been considered in the context of infant feeding decisions. Social class is strongly independently associated with breastfeeding (Foster *et al*, 1997) but the reasons are not well understood. A recent qualitative study among women in East London categorised them according to their confidence about, and commitment to, their chosen feeding method. Hoddinott & Pill (1999) state, *"When breastfeeding was witnessed as part of normal every day life by both the woman and her family and friends she was more confident in her own ability to breastfeed and committed to her decision. If breastfeeding had been seen only infrequently, and other people present had made negative comments, her reaction was less positive."* Thus, in addition to the strong independent relationship between a mother's own infant feeding experience and the practice she adopts for her child (Foster *et al*, 1997), social class may operate by creating a socio-cultural environment which either undermines or is conducive to breastfeeding. This may in turn affect the support given to less affluent women who decide to breastfeed. Health professionals may be less motivated to support women whose peer groups are less likely to breastfeed (McIntosh, 1985).

5.8.1.v *Psychosocial stress*
Psychosocial stress may affect parents' potential to care for their children. Capacity to parent children is now widely recognised to affect eating habits and, in consequence, the child's nutritional status (see Figure 5.4). Relative, rather than absolute, poverty has been consistently associated with poor psychosocial health (Wilkinson, 1999). Deprivation has also been consistently associated with increased prevalence of mental ill health (Eachus *et al*, 1996; Baker *et al*, 1997; Boyle *et al*, 1999). Baker *et al* (1997) found that depression among women 8 weeks pre- and post-partum was significantly more common among those living in rented accommodation who did not have access to a car.

5.8.1.vi *Smoking*
Smoking is highly correlated with social class (ONS, 1998b). It has been associated with reduced nutrient intake during pregnancy (section 5.4.1.iii) and is a strong predictor of low birth weight (Meis *et al*, 1997) (section 5.4.1.ii). Non-smoking has also been associated with healthier eating (Anderson & Hunt, 1992). In addition smoking during pregnancy has been associated with lower rates of breastfeeding initiation (Foster *et al*, 1997 and section 5.5.1.ii) and duration (Clements *et al*, 1997).

5.8.2 Maternal age
We have noted low maternal age to be associated with a number of adverse outcomes including:

• low uptake of folate supplements (section 5.3.1.ii)

• low nutrient intake during pregnancy (section 5.4.1.iii),

• low prevalence of breastfeeding (section 5.5.1.ii)

• early introduction of cow's milk (section 5.6.1.iv)

This section examines possible mechanisms.

5.8.2.i *Nutritional requirements*
Dietary reference values (DRV) for women aged 15-18 years are higher than those for older women in order to cover any additional requirements of adolescence (section 4.4.1). Despite this, younger pregnant women are likely to have lower intakes of nutrients (section 4.8.2), even after adjustment for social class. The explanation may be that younger mothers are less likely to have planned their pregnancy and may be less motivated to change their diet (Mathews *et al*, 2000).

68

5.8.2.ii *Income*

In some circumstances low maternal age is independently related to low income. This is so for lone parents dependent on welfare benefits (Dowler *et al*, 1995). IS and IBJSA allowances are lowest for people aged 16-18 years (Annex 2) who are only entitled under special circumstances. Pregnant women under 16 are not entitled to receive welfare foods (section 4.1.5.i).

5.8.2.iii *Cooking skills*

Women's confidence in cooking increases with age (Table 29). Younger women are more likely to regard cooking classes at school as an important source of learning, particularly those from lower social classes, though women from all groups primarily learn cooking skills from their mothers (Caraher *et al*, 1999).

Table 5.18: Percentage of women in each age group who are confident they can cook various food types (Health Education Authority, 1999)

Food type	16-19 years	20-24 years	25-34 years	35-44 years
White fish	40.2	61.6	76.2	85.4
Pulses	37.5	44.0	55.4	66.8
Chicken	64.6	81.8	92.0	96.3
Root vegetables	75.1	83.0	91.8	94.8

5.8.2.iv *Teenage pregnancy*

Great Britain has the highest rates of teenage pregnancy in Europe. Ninety per cent of pregnant teenagers receive IS and they are 25% more likely to give birth to a low birth weight baby (Social Exclusion Unit, 1999). See also sections 6.3.1.ii and 6.4.3.i.

5.8.3   Educational attainment

Low maternal educational attainment is confounded by low income and low maternal age yet some independent associations have been noted:

• low uptake of folic acid supplements (section 5.3.1.ii)

• low nutrient intake during pregnancy (section 5.4.1.iii)

• lower breastfeeding prevalence (section 5.5.1.ii)

• iron deficiency anaemia in children (section 5.6.1.iv)

• dental caries in children (section 5.6.3.ii)

5.8.3.i *The importance of health education*

Lack of information may not explain the relationship between maternal educational attainment and nutritional outcomes. Working class mothers in Glasgow were advised by their health visitor when to introduce solids but did so considerably earlier than recommended. The disadvantages of early weaning were not obvious to the mother who believed she knew best the needs of her child, and that solids gave the child a good "backing" (McIntosh, 1986). Early introduction had a definite purpose: solids were used to solve problems of a hungry child, or a child who would not sleep through the night (McIntosh, 1986). In contrast another study suggested that women who introduce solids early are less likely to have received formal information about the optimal timing of weaning (Savage et al, 1998).

Another Glasgow study showed that working class women based their decisions about breastfeeding not upon information about its benefits or the advantages of bottle-feeding but its social implications (McIntosh, 1985). They are more inclined to act upon the advice of lay people than professionals (McIntosh, 1985; Wylie & Verber, 1994). Other studies of food choice reveal that health information influences the decisions of low-income families to a lesser extent than socio-cultural norms, lack of resources and financial instability (Kennedy & Ling, 1997). Thus efforts to provide dietary education to women have failed to change dietary practice (Anderson & Campbell, 1995; Kennedy & Ling, 1997).

An alternative hypothesis has been proposed to explain the varying breastfeeding rates among women of differing educational attainment. Hoddinott & Pill (1999) proposed that "embodied knowledge" and "cognitive knowledge" are required to develop a skill such as breastfeeding: "*for women from lower socio-economic groups who learn skills through apprenticeship, embodied knowledge gained through exposure to breastfeeding may be more influential than theoretical knowledge. In contrast, women with higher educational qualifications are more familiar with learning and making decisions on the basis of theoretical knowledge*" (Hoddinott & Pill, 1999).

5.8.4   Ethnicity
Ethnicity has been independently associated with:

• increased incidence but shorter duration of breastfeeding (section 5.5.1.ii)

• childhood iron deficiency anaemia (section 5.6.1.iv)

• early introduction of cow's milk (section 5.6.1.iv)

• vitamin D deficiency in childhood and during pregnancy (sections 5.4.4.ii and 5.6.2.ii).

Lack of national data obviates full assessment of the contribution of ethnicity to nutritional vulnerability. Those available are confined to infant feeding practices and the vitamin D status of Asian children. There are no comparable data concerning the Afro-Caribbean population which is the second largest minority group.

5.8.4.i *Ethnicity and social class*

The broad effects of low socio-economic status on nutritional vulnerability have been highlighted in section 5.8.1.

Table 5.19 shows that higher proportions of ethnic minority populations are unemployed or in lower social class groups. The population of Indian origin however has a social class structure comparable to the white population. The proportion of household expenditure allocated to food reflects socio-economic status: it reaches 23% among Pakistani and Bangladeshi families, compared to 15% among Indian families and 17% of white families (Office of National Statistics, 1999c).

Table 5.19: Ethnic differences in social class (Nazroo, 1998)

	% population				
	White	Caribbean	Indian	Pakistani	Bangladeshi
I/II	35	22	32	20	11
IIIN	15	18	20	15	18
IIIM	31	30	22	32	32
IV/V	20	30	26	33	40
Unemployed	11	24	15	38	42

5.8.4.ii *Traditional diets*

The traditional diets of some ethnic minority groups may place young children at risk of nutritional deficiencies. Dietary characteristics of potential importance are shown in Table 5.20. The Afro-Caribbean diet is not included but in general it presents a lower proportion of dietary energy as fat (Bush *et al*, 1997) and is richer in micronutrients (Dowler *et al*, 1995). The extremely restrictive diets of particular sub-groups, for example Rastafarians, may be limiting in some nutrients such as vitamin D (Department of Health, 1998).

Table 5.20: Key characteristics of ethnic diets (Bush *et al*, 1997)

Bangladeshi	Pakistani	Indian
• Halal meat	• Wheat staple eaten primarily as chapatis (high phytate content)	• Punjabi Indians – wheat staple eaten primarily as chapatis (high phytate content)
	• Halal meat	• Strict Hindus –vegetarians associated with low intakes of vitamin B12 (Abraham *et al*, 1987).
		• Sikhs – use of ghee (unfortified fat)

5.8.4.iii *Availability of Halal complementary foods*

Commercially produced Halal complementary foods which may be required by Muslims are not widely available. This may explain the narrower range of complementary foods (Thomas & Avery, 1997) and high proportion of sweet, poorly fortified commercial foods consumed by Bangladeshi children (Aukett & Wharton, 1989; Bush *et al*, 1997).

5.8.4.iv *Access to information and health services*
The National Health and Lifestyles Survey of Black and Minority Ethnic Groups in England (Rudat, 1994) showed that 85% of Indian, 72% of Pakistani and 59% of Bengali adults spoke English. The proportions were lower among women and older people. Only 21% of Bangladeshi women aged 30-49 and 10% of those aged 50-74 years spoke English. A study in Cardiff noted that those Asian women with low 25-hydroxyvitamin D levels at delivery were those who could not speak English (Alfaham *et al*, 1995). Moreover, Bangladeshi children have been shown to have poorer iron status if the mother did not speak English (Lawson *et al*, 1998). Two small studies have correlated the language problems of Bangladeshi women with poor comprehension of information concerning infant feeding (cited in Bush *et al*, 1997). Similar observations have been made among Vietnamese mothers in London (Sharma *et al*, 1994). In the national "Asian Feeding Survey" sample no Bangladeshi and Pakistani mothers gave publicity, media or advice as reasons for avoiding certain foods for their toddlers, whereas 10% of white mothers did (Thomas & Avery, 1997). It is unclear whether this difference would remain after controlling for social class.

Ethnic minorities appear to make more use of primary healthcare services (Rudat, 1994) though this appears to reflect a greater prevalence of ill health (Nazroo, 1997). Ethnic minority groups have reported a lower quality of service than the general population; for example a third of Bangladeshis, compared to about one-eighth of the general population, felt that the GP spent inadequate time with them (Rudat, 1994).

5.8.4.v *Short duration of breastfeeding*
Mothers of Asian background initiate breastfeeding more often but by 4 months show a prevalence similar to that of white mothers (section 5.5.1.ii). The groups studied gave different reasons for stopping: Asian mothers were more likely to report "insufficient milk", or the "baby not sucking", whereas white mothers were more likely to report painful breasts or nipples. Indian and white mothers were more likely than those of Bangladeshi or Pakistani origin to report that breastfeeding took too long or that they needed to return to work (Thomas & Avery, 1997). It is not possible to determine the extent to which these factors operate independently of social class. The underlying causes of these patterns seem poorly understood but erosion of family support and advice networks may be responsible (Bush *et al*, 1997).

5.8.5   Conclusions

Low social class (section 5.8.1) may be associated with adverse nutritional outcomes because:

• Lack of money restricts food choice and transport to cheaper retail outlets (sections 5.8.1.i and 5.8.1.ii). This seems likely to be the predominant factor explaining associations with social class.

• Living conditions may restrict access to cooking facilities (section 5.8.1.iii).

72

- Socio-cultural norms may be at variance with optimal dietary practices (section 5.8.1.iv).

Low maternal age (section 5.8.2) may be associated with adverse nutritional outcomes because:

- Young women have a lower entitlement to benefits: mothers <16 years have no entitlement at all (section 5.8.2.ii).

- Young women have increased nutritional requirements but lower nutrient intakes (section 5.8.2.i).

- Young women are less confident about their ability to prepare food (section 5.8.2.iii).

Low educational attainment (section 5.8.3) is associated with adverse nutritional outcomes for reasons which are less clear. The association is not simply a consequence of lack of information.

Ethnicity (section 5.8.4) may be associated with adverse nutritional outcomes because:

- People from some ethnic groups are likely to be poorer (section 5.8.4.i).

- Culturally acceptable diets may restrict intake of some nutrients (section 5.8.4.ii).

- Specialised (e.g. Halal) weaning foods are not widely available (section 5.8.4.iii).

- Language problems reduce access to information (section 5.8.4.iv).

5.9   Conclusions

This chapter examined evidence for the existence of nutritionally vulnerable groups of women and children in the United Kingdom. For each specified adverse nutritional outcome the groups who are most at risk have been identified in order to inform any potential targeted intervention.   There is little doubt that associations between poverty and poor nutritional status persist. Specific risk factors include low income and social class, low maternal age, poor educational attainment and ethnicity. These place affected groups of the population at risk in the following circumstances:

- **Conception**. Inadequate intake of folic acid places child bearing women at risk of neural tube defects (section 5.3.1.i). Women least likely to meet RNI for folate at the time of conception are those of low socio-economic status and those who have unplanned pregnancies. The latter group includes a disproportionate proportion of young women, particularly teenagers (section 5.3.1.ii).

- **Pregnancy**. Low birthweight is observed more frequently among the socially deprived though in a United Kingdom context there is little evidence that low nutrient intake is directly responsible (section 5.4.1.ii). Younger women, particularly those who smoke, have poorer diets during pregnancy. Teenage mothers, who have higher nutritional requirements and lower benefit provision, are at greatest risk (sections 5.4.1.iii; 5.4.5.i).

- **Infancy**. Optimal infant nutrition is achieved in babies who are breastfed exclusively for their first four to six months after which complementary foods should be gradually introduced (section 4.6.1.i). A significant proportion of women do not initiate breastfeeding (particularly younger women on low incomes). Many do not breastfeed exclusively or stop early (particularly Asian mothers) (section 5.5.1.ii). Early introduction of solids is more likely among babies who are not breastfed (section 5.5.2.ii). Early introduction of, and prolonged dependence on, liquid cow's milk is more likely among children from Asian families and children of young mothers (sections 5.5.2.ii and 5.6.1.iv).

- Failure to thrive (FTT) affects a small proportion of children and has long-term consequences (section 5.5.3.iii). It has its origins in infancy though may not be apparent until later. Identifying groups of the population at risk is not easy due to the complexity of contributing factors. Although these are more common in households suffering from socio-economic deprivation FTT may occur in all social groups (section 5.5.3.iv).

- **Early childhood.** Iron deficiency anaemia is the commonest nutritional deficiency in early childhood. It affects children from ethnic minorities disproportionately (section 5.6.1.iv). Early introduction of cow's milk, and prolonged dependence on it at the expense of a more varied weaning diet, are key contributory factors (section 5.6.1.iii).

- Vitamin D deficiency affects a significant proportion of children of Asian origin and while this group of the population have higher intakes of supplements, a considerable number remain vulnerable to deficiency (section 5.6.2.ii). Maternal deficiency may also place some Asian children at risk (section 5.4.4.ii).

- Dental caries affects a large proportion of children, particularly those fed with a bottle or those who consume sugary foods frequently. Poorer children are at greatest risk (section 5.6.3.ii).

- **Later childhood.** Childhood fatness is becoming an increasing problem among school children. Children at risk are those whose parents are obese and those who have high birth weights (section 5.7.1.iv). Dietary factors are not strong predictors (section 5.7.1.iii).

- Adolescent girls are at particular risk of low intakes of minerals and undertake least physical exercise (section 5.7.2).

- Schoolchildren from families in receipt of benefit are at particular risk of missing breakfast (section 5.7.2).

These nutritional problems are evident in spite of existing benefit provisions and national health promotion programmes. Thus, the evidence in this chapter represents existing unmet needs. Vulnerability would undoubtedly be much more extensive in the absence of existing welfare provision. Infants and young children could particularly be adversely affected if the provisions of the Welfare Food Scheme were removed. Thus interventions addressing the vulnerabilities highlighted in this chapter should not be regarded as *alternatives* to the current Scheme but rather as *additions*.

Table 5.21: Consumption of folic acid

Indicators	Name of survey	Survey details	England and Wales	Scotland	Northern Ireland
INTAKE					
% non pregnant women aged 19-50 consuming folate <RNI	The Dietary and Nutritional Survey of British Adults 1990 (Gregory et al, 1990)	Including intakes from supplements	47		
% non pregnant women aged 19-50 consuming folate <LRNI			4		
PRECONCEPTIONAL SUPPLEMENTS					
% pregnant women reporting they had taken folic acid supplements preconception	Sutcliffe et al, 1993, 1994 Wild et al, 1997	Consecutive women making their first hospital antenatal visit in Leeds General Infirmary 3 consecutive years	2 (1993) 18 (1994) 31 (1996)		
	Mathews et al, 1998	Study of 963 pregnant women recruited from district general hospital in S England	24[1]		
POST CONCEPTIONAL SUPPLEMENTS					
% post partum women reporting that they had taken supplements during early pregnancy	Infant Feeding Survey 1995 (Foster et al, 1997)	Retrospective questioning	50	46	54
% pregnant women reporting they had taken folic acid supplements during first trimester of pregnancy	Smith et al, 1994	507 women attending first antenatal clinic at University of Wales Cardiff for one month period	3		
	Mathews et al, 1998	See above	63[1]		

[1] >350mg folic acid

76

Table 5.22: Average intakes of nutrients reported in British studies of pregnant women

Study	Energy (MJ)	Protein (g)	Sodium (mg)	Potassium (mg)	Calcium (mg)	Magnesium (mg)	Phosphorous (mg)	Chloride (mg)	Iron (mg)	Zinc (mg)	Copper (mg)	Selenium (µg)
DRV[1]	8.9-9.5	51	1600	3500	700	270	550-625	2500	14.8	7.0	1.0-1.2	60
Anderson &Campbell (1995)[2]	9.5	75.9	3025	3400	1003	310	1350	4664	12.7	9.6	1.6	
Haste et al (1991)[3]	7.4	65			840				8.5	7.7		
Mathews & Neil (1998b)[4]**	8.5				936.2				17.5	8.4		53.5
Rogers et al (1998b)[5]*	7.04	55.2	2363		899	223			9.2	7.48		
Wynn et al (1991)[6]*	7.1	64.5	2078	2513	775	203	1055	3237	9.82	8.45	1.17	
Abraham et al (1987)[7]*					1184				10.6			
Eaton et al (1984)[8]*	6.9-7.8	51-60	1700-2000	1800-2300	762-956	219-255	914-1116	2800-3200	11-12	6.4-7.6	1.1-1.3	
Schofield et al (1989)[9]*	7.9	68			908				9.4			
Robinson et al (1996)[10]*	8.0	69			884				10.1	8.0	1.0	
Black et al (1986)[11]**	8.0				1100	260	1300		11	9	1.6	

Study	Thiamin (mg)	Riboflavin (mg)	Nicotinic acid equiv (mg)	Vitamin C (mg)	Vitamin B6 (mg)	Vitamin B12 (µg)	Total folate (µg)	Vitamin A (RE µg)	Vitamin D (µg)
DRV	0.9	1.4	13-14	50	1.2	1.5	600	700	10
Anderson &Campbell (1995)	1.4	21.96	19.4	73.7	1.4	3.7	155.6	742	2.2
Haste et al (1991)	1.08	1.6		41	0.98		126		8.5
Mathews & Neil (1998b)	1.73	1.92		90.8	4.1		334.8	863	2.9
Rogers et al (1998b)	1.27	1.64	28.3	57.6	1.68		220	886	
Wynn et al (1991)	0.94	1.41	26.1	98.3	1.19	3.81	167	597	4.33
Abraham et al (1987)	1.2	1.78	22.7	89		2.7	161	1160	1.41
Eaton et al (1984)	1.0-1.2	1.1-1.4	16.4-18.5	44-65	1.0-1.1	1.9-3.0	119-134	727-856	0.9-1.2
Schofield et al (1989)				44.6			115	2843	
Robinson et al (1996)	1.4	1.6	16.7	65	1.7	3.8	205	678	2.0
Black et al (1986)	1.2	2.0	32.8	65	1.1	7	165	2576	1.7

[1] DRV means Estimated Average Requirement for energy and Reference Nutrient Intakes for other nutrients
[2] non-intervention group mean
[3] lowest mean intake from non-smoking or smoking group at 36 week gestation
[4] total study group mean
[5] lowest mean of smoking and s-e groups
[6] median of mothers whose babies weighed <=2500g at birth
[7] mean intake of Asian pregnant women – 7 day recall
[8] range of means for weighed intakes at 18, 23, 28, 33 and 38 weeks gestation
[9] mean weighed intake at 32-40 weeks gestation
[10] median intake for pregnant women in Edinburgh measured by food diary at 16 weeks gestation
[11] mean of pregnant women (4-9 months) from manual social classes

* nutrients from supplements not included   ** nutrients from supplements included.   Shaded cells show average intakes which fall below DRV (EAR for energy; RNI for other nutrients).

Chapter 6: Effect of the Welfare Food Scheme on beneficiaries

6.1   Introduction

The inherent difficulty in evaluating the effects of the Welfare Food Scheme on targeted recipients is identifying a suitable control group. Although the Welfare Food Scheme has been in place since the 1940s, it is a public health rather than research programme and has never been formally evaluated as an intervention. Households on Income Support (IS), Income Based JSA (IBJSA) or Family Credit (FC), nursery school children and severely disabled children are population sub-groups with diverse characteristics which include a number of social, biological and environmental risk factors. With a few exceptions national studies have not specifically analysed nutritional outcome according to receipt of WFS benefits. As a result we have often had to use social class, receipt of DSS benefits and other characteristics as proxies for receipt of WFS benefits. This clearly poses problems.

In this chapter we consider factors relevant to evaluating the impact of the WFS including access, uptake, unintended use and abuse of the scheme (Figure 6). In view of the difficulty of identifying both WFS recipients and controls we then examine nutritional and economic effects on probable beneficiaries by addressing two questions:

- If all the intended recipients consumed their entire allowance what is the Scheme's potential for preventing nutritional vulnerability?

- If the provisions of the scheme were removed, what might the consequences be?

Figure 6: Steps in the process of reviewing the effect of the Scheme on beneficiaries

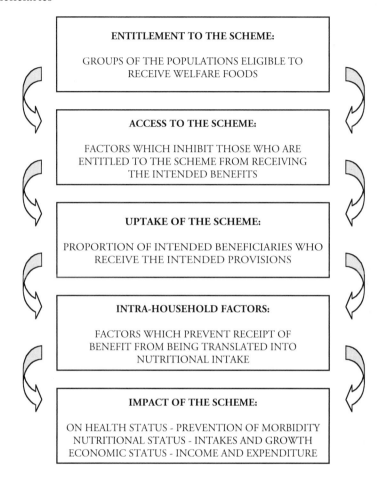

ENTITLEMENT TO THE SCHEME:

GROUPS OF THE POPULATIONS ELIGIBLE TO RECEIVE WELFARE FOODS

ACCESS TO THE SCHEME:

FACTORS WHICH INHIBIT THOSE WHO ARE ENTITLED TO THE SCHEME FROM RECEIVING THE INTENDED BENEFITS

UPTAKE OF THE SCHEME:

PROPORTION OF INTENDED BENEFICIARIES WHO RECEIVE THE INTENDED PROVISIONS

INTRA-HOUSEHOLD FACTORS:

FACTORS WHICH PREVENT RECEIPT OF BENEFIT FROM BEING TRANSLATED INTO NUTRITIONAL INTAKE

IMPACT OF THE SCHEME:

ON HEALTH STATUS - PREVENTION OF MORBIDITY
NUTRITIONAL STATUS - INTAKES AND GROWTH
ECONOMIC STATUS - INCOME AND EXPENDITURE

6.2   Access to and uptake of the scheme

We use the term "access" to describe the process by which tokens and listed products are distributed and particularly try to identify groups of intended beneficiaries whose access may be constrained inadvertently. By "uptake" we mean the result of the process; that is the actual numbers of tokens used and the volume of listed products distributed. There are no data about the quantity of WFS listed products eventually consumed by intended beneficiaries, as opposed to other family members.

6.2.1   Access

Access to welfare foods is potentially restricted by obstacles to:

- receiving tokens

- exchanging tokens

- obtaining vitamins

- using milk and vitamins (for example a medical contra-indication or cultural preference)

6.2.1.i   *Information*

There are a number of sources of information about the WFS intended to inform potential beneficiaries of entitlements:

- The Scheme is widely described in Social Security and Benefit materials (in a variety of languages) intended for those who claim IS, IBJSA or Family Credit.

- The Scheme has produced its own information leaflet (only in English). This is currently available from DSS offices, public libraries, all NHS trust clinics and DH Stores.

- Information about the Scheme for nursery milk providers is provided through two key channels: Local Social Services Authorities with whom day care providers have to register and Local Education Authorities (Education Authorities in Scotland) who provide state nursery education. Day care providers are advised to contact the WFRU to receive a leaflet and application form.

- Eligible parents of disabled children are informed of their entitlement in all the existing material on disability benefits.

- A free national telephone HelpLine is in place to answer queries concerning the Scheme and to report fraud.

Groups at risk of not receiving information include:

- Pregnant women receiving IBJSA who have never received milk tokens before. They may not inform DSS of their pregnancy until 11 weeks before their expected date of confinement (29 weeks of gestation) when they become eligible for IS by virtue of being unable to work.

- Those who do not speak or read English (see Section 5.8.4.iv) may be particularly at risk because they may not have had access to appropriate information materials.

- Private nurseries are the other major group of providers of nursery milk. There is no information specifically targeted at them.

Information which may negatively affect access to the Scheme:

- Public health warnings about the risks associated with high vitamin A intake during pregnancy have been reported anecdotally to deter women from taking up free vitamin supplements which contain vitamin A.

6.2.1.ii *Physical access*

Receipt of tokens and chosen products
Recipients of IS and IBJSA are eligible to receive the tokens automatically on receipt of their monetary benefit. Social Security Benefits can be paid at a post office (usually fortnightly) or can be paid directly into the recipient's bank account by Automated Credit Transfer.

- If tokens are received directly from the post office, the recipient states at each visit which type of milk she requires.

- At least 10% of households receive their benefit by Automated Credit Transfer (DSS, 1999a,1999b) and their tokens are sent by post each month by the local DSS. The local DSS office is required by the Scheme to ask the beneficiary the type of milk token required or otherwise to send liquid milk tokens.

Most formulas and vitamins are distributed through maternity and child health clinics. Outlets should be adequate for local beneficiary needs, should be suitably located within distances of beneficiaries' homes and should offer convenient opening times (NHS Executive, 1995). In recent years some authorities and trusts have chosen to make arrangements for local distribution through non-clinic outlets, either wholly or partly replacing clinics. Local community pharmacies, local retailers or GP's premises have been the choice in some areas.

Exchanging liquid milk tokens
Liquid milk tokens can be exchanged by any shop, supermarket or milkman who will accept them (there are more than 20,000 such outlets in the UK). If exchanged at supermarket chains, seven pints must be obtained in one go which may cause difficulties of storage or transport (Wharfe, 1999). Furthermore there has been some indication that the full value of the tokens can not be obtained in some smaller shops (Wharfe, 1999) to which low income households may have easiest access (section 5.8.1.ii).

Obtaining vitamins
Breastfeeding women or mothers of children aged 1-4 years may have particular difficulties obtaining vitamins. In the experience of the Panel, most baby clinics are run by general practitioners, many of whom are not based in health centres where welfare foods are available, though national data to support this observation could not be identified. Unless mothers are making a journey to a

health centre for formula milk, they may not be able to obtain their free vitamins. Welfare Food Scheme vitamins cannot be bought at pharmacies and were difficult for GPs to prescribe because they were omitted from the British National Formulary for several years prior to 1999. GPs may in the past have prescribed more expensive proprietary brands. In 1998, 230,000 prescriptions for *Abidec* and *Dalivit* were issued although these supplements are intended for a broader range of clinical applications.

Pregnant women similarly will have difficulty obtaining vitamin supplements if they are not regularly attending a clinic. A national survey in England and Wales indicated that 18% of women did not make their first contact with the health services to discuss maternity care until they were 12-20 weeks pregnant (Audit Commission, 1998). Those who know about the vitamins and claim their entitlement can receive two 10ml bottles of drops every 13 weeks (if they are pregnant or have a child under five) or two packs of 45 tablets every 13 weeks until their child reaches one year if breastfeeding (NHS Executive, 1995,1996).

Whilst the provision of infant formula and vitamins at health centres may disadvantageously limit access to these products, a potential benefit is that mothers who do attend to collect their entitlement can be seen opportunistically by the health visitor (Hall, 1995). Some of these women may otherwise be difficult to locate (Dodds, 1999). Moreover, increasing access to infant formula (for example by making it available through pharmacies) must be balanced against the risks of commercial influence and lack of professional infant feeding support (Hall, 1995).

Nursery milk
The following types of day care providers are eligible to apply to provide welfare milk:

- a registered child minder

- a registered day care provider

- a local authority to the extent that it is providing day care under Section 18 of the Children Act 1989 or under section 12 of the Social Work (Scotland) Act 1968(b)

- an exempt school (a school or play centre which though providing day care is exempt from registering with the local authority under section 71 (1) (b) of the Children Act 1989)

- an exempt establishment to the extent that day care is being provided to children as part of the activities of the establishment only because the children are children of persons carrying on or employed to work at that establishment (a home or other establishment which though providing day care is exempt from registering with the local authority under section 71 (1) (b) of the Children Act 1989)

These categories cover the full range of facilities offering day care. Only those not legally registered are ineligible to register for the Scheme with WFRU (section 3.2.4). Only children under 5 years old who attend a day care facility for more than two hours in a day have access to nursery milk. Infants are eligible to receive formula rather than liquid milk.

Disabled children
Entitlement assumes that the child is not a registered pupil at a school because of a mental or physical disability (section 3.2.5). In total 36 disabled children were recipients of the Scheme in 1998 in Great Britain and none is currently registered in Northern Ireland.

6.2.1.iii *Special medical circumstances and cultural preferences*
Some individuals are eligible for the Scheme but for some reason cannot consume the welfare foods provided. Those affected may include:

- *Infants who require a special type of infant formula for medical or cultural reasons.* Follow-on formulas, soya based formulas and nutrient-enriched formulas for pre-term or low birth weight babies are not provided under the Scheme and must be purchased or prescribed. In 1998, 355,000 prescriptions were issued for soya formulas but it is not known what proportion were given to individuals entitled to Welfare Foods. This represents an alarming misuse of soya formula for which genuine medical indications are rare. Soya milk has been shown to contain high levels of phytoestrogens (the effects of which are poorly understood) (MAFF, 1996) and phytates which can reduce the bioavailability of iron (Hurrell *et al*, 1992). A formula based upon cow's milk protein hydrolysates is preferred for the treatment of food allergies (Høst *et al*, 1999).

- *Babies born prematurely* may have increased nutritional needs (section 5.5.4) requiring individual prescription of nutrient enriched formula or dietary supplements. Elsewhere we also drew attention to the anomaly of effectively withdrawing this group's entitlement to formula at an earlier developmental stage (section 5.5.4).

- *Pregnant or breastfeeding women who are lactose intolerant* or normally restrict their intake of dairy products. Jejunal biopsy studies suggest that about 5% of people of European origin and up to 75% of the non-white population are deficient in lactase. It is suggested that about half of these may develop symptoms on drinking milk (Ferguson *et al*, 1984).

- *Children with physical disability* who have difficulty eating derive more benefit from a nutrient enriched specialist feed than liquid cow's milk.

- *Children from low income families who have special nutritional needs.* Children with certain medical conditions (e.g. cystic fibrosis, chronic renal failure or congenital heart disease) may have increased nutritional needs not necessarily met by prescribable products. They may therefore have limited flexibility of choice and by default have need to purchase more expensive normal foods. The Disability Living Allowance does not currently assess such special nutritional needs.

6.2.2   Uptake

Data available to evaluate the uptake of the Scheme include:

1. The number of tokens issued;

2. the number of tokens exchanged for liquid milk ;

3. the number of units of vitamins and formula claimed by Health Authorities / Health Boards;

4. the number of units of reduced price formula claimed by Health Authorities/ Health Boards for families on Family Credit;

5. the value of reimbursements made for nursery milk;

6. the reported receipt of milk tokens and vitamins (not gathered by the Scheme but by several national surveys).

These data do not provide a complete measure of the use of the Scheme.

6.2.2.i   *Infant formula*

DSS/WFS data

DSS data on the numbers of infants in households receiving IS, IBJSA and FC are shown in Table 6.1. Data from the Welfare Food Scheme show that the average number of tins of formula dispensed through the Scheme each week in the first quarter of 1999 exactly balanced DSS data on the number of eligible infants. This suggests that:

• All eligible women received tokens and exchanged them within the 4-week expiry period.

• All mothers of children under 1 year of age exchanged their tokens for infant formula.

Yet these findings are difficult to reconcile with two observations:

• Some (admittedly few) women would have chosen to breastfeed and should have collected liquid milk.

• A number of women deliberately chose to give liquid cow's milk to their baby before 1 year of age (see below).

One explanation may be that some women continue to collect infant formula beyond the baby's first birthday (section 7.2.1.ii). Alternatively the explanation lies in limitations of the DSS and WFS data. Whilst Health Authorities / Boards usually reclaim the value of formula from the Scheme on a quarterly basis they may delay by 3-6 months. Similarly beneficiaries may delay exchanging tokens. This means that quarterly data on IS/IBJSA claimants from DSS could on occasion over- or underestimate the number of tins claimed from WFS during the same period.

Table 6.1 also shows that only 21% of those on FC purchased low-cost formula from the health centre. It is not known why the remaining 79% did not take advantage of the reduced rate available under the Scheme. Possible reasons include:

• Remaining mothers were breastfeeding, though this seems unlikely.

• The cost of getting to the Health Centre outweighs the saving on shop prices.

• People on FC are not aware of their entitlement to low-cost milk.

Table 6.1: Uptake of infant formula by eligible infants in England

	Number	Source of data
INCOME SUPPORT / INCOME BASED JSA		
Infants whose parents receive Income Support or Income Based JSA (February, 1999) in England	130,000	DSS (1999a,b)
Beneficiaries who claimed for infant formula by Income Support / JSA households (first quarter 1999) in England[1]	130,366	WFS
% eligible recipients who exchanged tokens	100	Extrapolated
FAMILY CREDIT		
Infants whose parents receive Family Credit in England (February, 1999)	65,000	DSS (1999c)
Reduced price infant formula purchased by Family Credit households in England[2]	13,661	WFS
% eligible recipients who obtained reduced price formula	21	Extrapolated

[1] total number of tins claimed by Health Authorities for January – March divided by thirteen to obtain the weekly total
[2] total number of reduced price tins claimed by Health Authorities for January – March divided by thirteen to obtain the weekly total

Data from beneficiary reports
Data from surveys of groups eligible for the Scheme portrays a different picture of uptake. The "Asian Feeding Survey" indicated that 6% of white women receiving IS did not receive milk tokens (Table 6.2).

Table 6.2 and Table 6.3 show that uptake differs between ethnic groups. A greater proportion of Asian mothers reported not receiving tokens when the baby was 9 weeks old, though this difference narrowed as the child got older. The authors suggested some mothers may not have known they had received milk tokens because their husbands received the benefit and did the shopping (Thomas & Avery, 1997).

Table 6.3 shows that most of those white mothers who received tokens exchanged them at the clinic or chemist (84% at 9 weeks), suggesting they were exchanged for infant formula rather than liquid milk. This proportion fell to 57% when the baby was 9 months old (Table 6.3) (Thomas & Avery, 1997). The 1995 Infant Feeding Survey revealed a similar picture: at 4 months after delivery, 73% of mothers exchanged their milk tokens at a clinic (only 46% in Northern Ireland) (Foster *et al*, 1997). These findings are compatible with the previously noted similarities between ethnic groups in the prevalence of breastfeeding at 9 weeks of age (see Section 5.5.1.ii).

Because formula can only be obtained from a clinic or chemist, the data suggest a reduction in the proportion of mothers obtaining formula as their children get older. Possible explanations are:

- Reduced use of infant formula in the volumes allocated and use of tokens for liquid cow's milk for other family members.

- Early transition to liquid milk. It has been suggested that early transition to cow's milk occurs because it seems easier to prepare and feed (Daly *et al*, 1996).

- Difficulties in accessing formula from the Health Centres.

- Tokens are fraudulently used for other items .

Table 6.2: Uptake of milk tokens by mothers of infants from Asian and white families who received Income Support (Thomas and Avery, 1997)[1]

	Age of child	Bangladeshi %	Pakistani %	Indian %	White
Free milk or reduced price milk Neither	9 weeks	87 13	90 10	88 13	94 6
Free milk or reduced price milk Neither	5 months	95 6	94 6	87 12	95 5
Free milk or reduced price milk Neither	9 months	94 6	95 5	90 9	95 5

[1] These data may not be entirely accurate as mothers were asked if they had received "tokens for free or reduced price formula". Tokens are not given, however, for reduced price formula and mothers on income support can only receive tokens for free formula.

Table 6.3: Percentage of milk tokens exchanged at the clinic and chemist by ethnic group (Thomas & Avery, 1997)

	CLINIC				CHEMIST			
Age	Bangladeshi	Pakistani	Indian	White	Bangladeshi	Pakistani	Indian	White
9 weeks	83	81	69	72	5	8	10	12
5 months	80	77	73	70	7	10	8	12
9 months	66	50	56	49	5	8	8	8

6.2.2.ii   *Liquid milk*

DSS/WFS Data

Using data from Table 6.4 it can be calculated that all (102% [2]) individuals entitled only to liquid milk (pregnant women and children aged 1-4 years) exchanged milk tokens. This calculation assumes that none of those with a child under 1 year exchanged their tokens for liquid milk though, as we have shown (section 6.2.2.i), many do. The figure of 102% must therefore overestimate consumption by pregnant women and children 1-4 years of age. DSS and WFS data cannot be expected to match exactly because retail suppliers are allowed two years in which to claim reimbursement. Moreover, claims cannot be made during the quarter in which the milk was supplied.

Data on the number of tokens circulated in 1998 indicate that up to 9% of tokens issued were not returned. These may have expired or been lost, or the recipient may not have known how to exchange them. It is unclear whether the data include double-counting incurred through replacement of lost tokens (Welfare Foods Unit, [personal communication]). These figures are difficult to reconcile with information in Table 6.1 and Table 6.4 which implies that all eligible persons received milk and, by implication, all issued tokens were exchanged.

Data from beneficiary reports

Unlike the national infant feeding surveys, NDNS did not quantify receipt of tokens for liquid milk. However, 4% of the children studied in households who received IS did not consume whole or semi-skimmed cow's milk. This suggests a small proportion did not receive milk allocated to them by the Scheme (Gregory *et al*, 1995).

A small study of pregnant women on IS who were all eligible for WFS benefit showed that only 76% were receiving milk tokens (Maternity Alliance, 1995). Another looked at receipt of milk tokens in IS households with a child under 5 years of age. It did not distinguish between tokens for formula and those for liquid cow's milk but indicated that individuals from large or non-white households are least likely to report receiving their liquid milk token entitlement (Table 6.5). These findings require cautious interpretation because assumptions about household composition were made (Research Surveys of Great Britain, 1989).

---

[2] (725,093/55,000+657,000)

Table 6.4: Uptake of liquid milk and vitamins by those eligible on Income Support and Income Based JSA in Great Britain

	Source of data	Number
Pregnant women receiving Income Support or Income Based JSA (February 1999)	DSS, 1999 a,b	55,000
Children aged 0-12 months in households receiving Income Support or Income Based JSA (February 1999)	DSS, 1999 a,b	151,000
Children aged 1-4 years in households receiving Income Support or Income Based JSA (February 1999)	DSS, 1999 a,b	657,000
Vitamins given out in the first quarter of 1999[2]: *10ml bottles of vitamin drops* *containers of 45 tablets*	WFS	12,267 (drops) 917 (tablets)
Average number of claimed tokens per week January – March 1999[1]	WFS	725,093

[1] The number of milk tokens exchanged for the month divided by four to obtain the weekly number. Tokens can be claimed for reimbursement up to two years after their date of issue thus, tokens claimed in January – March will not be an exact representation of those exchanged during that period by beneficiaries.

[2] The number of vitamins given out is equivalent to the number claimed for by Health Authorities/Health Boards. Health Authorities/Health Boards usually claim on a quarterly basis. Data on vitamins claimed may not be an exact representation of vitamins actually given out during the quarter.

Table 6.5: Receipt of liquid milk tokens by household type for households receiving Income Support and eligible for welfare foods (RSGB, 1989)*

Reporting receiving tokens for liquid milk	Ethnicity		Household composition		Household size			Age of parent responsible for child care	
	White	Non-white	Single parent	Two parent	2-3	4-5	6+	16-24	>25
Yes	98	92	99	93	98	100	81	97	95
No	2	6	1	5	2	-	14	3	3
Don't know / can't remember	-	3	-	2	-	-	5	-	2

* Assumes that the numbers of children under a year are equally distributed between household types and that the proportion of mothers who decide to exchange tokens for formula was similar in all households with a child under one year

6.2.2.iii *Vitamins*

DSS/WFS data

Table 6.4 shows the number of units of vitamin drops and tablets dispensed. A *conservative* estimate of the potential number to be dispensed can be made by assuming that each Scheme beneficiary would collect one bottle of drops (a 1 month supply) per quarter, and all mothers would claim tablets rather than drops. On that basis supply data suggest that only 1.4% of those eligible received any vitamin drops *at all* each quarter. The number of tablets dispensed was also extremely small, representing only 0.6% of mothers. Many Health Authorities / Health Boards distributed none at all.

Data from beneficiary reports

The NDNS data on reported supplement intake for children aged 1½- 4½ years are shown in Table 6.6. Only 2% of children from IS households (all eligible for free vitamins under the WFS) reported consumption. Indeed eligible children were even less likely than non-eligible children to receive vitamin drops.

Two surveys have reported on the uptake of free vitamin supplements by pregnant women receiving IS or IBJSA. The Maternity Alliance survey of pregnant women on IS showed that 12% took free vitamins though 32% knew about them (Maternity Alliance, 1995). A recent study in Portsmouth indicated that only 2 of the 727 pregnant women in the sample reported taking free ACD supplements despite 10% of the households not receiving an income (Mathews, 1999, personal communication).

Table 6.6: Use of dietary supplements during the four-day dietary record by socio-economic status of family (Gregory _et al_, 1995).

Socio-economic status of family	Percentage who took supplements during the 4-day dietary record			
	No. of children	Any type of supplement %	Vitamins A,C & D (not welfare vitamins) %	Welfare vitamin drops (A,C,D) %
Receiving Income Support	_456_	11	3	2
Receiving Family Credit	_117_	18	4	4
Non-welfare social class I – III non-manual	_613_	25	7	5
Non-welfare social class III - V manual	_503_	14	5	3
All children	_1675_	17	5	3

6.2.2.iv _Nursery Milk_

Data from WFS / DfEE

Table 6.4 indicates the proportion of children under 5 years of age who attend daycare facilities eligible for welfare milk provision. In England, in the first quarter of 1999, claims for nursery milk equated with provision of 1/3 pint of liquid milk once-a-day for five days a week to 536,409[1] children (approximately 20% of children aged 1-4 years), and 1/3 pint of infant formula for 593[2] children under 1 year of age. This represents about half the total number of children attending day care (see Table 6.7). The true number of children receiving any welfare milk may be greater because many attend on a part-time basis. We have not been able to determine the proportion of these children eligible on other grounds for WFS milk because there are no data on the proportion of attenders from households claiming IS, IBJSA or FC.

Data from beneficiary reports

The NDNS of children aged 1½-4½ years showed that two-thirds of children in the sample attended a play group, nursery or childminder. Half of the whole sample had a meal at the day care facility, 16% only had a snack and 2% had nothing to eat (Gregory _et al_, 1995).

---

[1] payments for liquid milk made for the quarter divided by the average cost of a third of a pint of milk and divided by 65 days (5 days / week).

[2] payments for formula milk divided by the average high street cost of formula powder to make a third of a pint of milk and divided by 65 days (5 days / week).

Table 6.7: Children in day care in England

Type of day care provider	Type of facility	Number of facilities	Number of places for children under five	Percentage of estimated under five population in 1997 (ONS, 1999b)
Registered childminder[1]		91,859	180,369	5.8
Registered day care provider[1]	Day nurseries Play groups	6,100 15,600	203,000 381,200	19
Local authority providing day care[1]	Day nurseries Play groups	500 50	18,670 1,200	0.6
Exempt school*	**Maintained** Nursery school, nursery classes in primary schools Infant classes in primary schools Special schools **Private** Private and voluntary Independent	6,673 Na Na Na Na	366,914 355,090 5,395 95,100** 54,491	12 11 0.1 3.0 1.8

[1] Data refers to number of places in March1998 (DfEE, 1999a)   * The data relates to the number of children in January 1999 rather than the number of places (DfEE, 1999b)   ** Data for voluntary school places are not available, Na means data not available

6.2.2.v *Milk for disabled children*

Only 36 disabled children aged 5-16 years are currently registered on the Scheme in Great Britain. They suffer from a range of medical conditions as diverse as myalgic encephalitis (ME), cancer and Down's Syndrome. The estimated cost of "buying out" current beneficiaries assuming that they would continue to receive a pint of milk per day until they reached the age of 16 has been estimated to be £20,000 (WFS, 1999).We have not been able to ascertain the number of eligible disabled children who do not claim.

6.2.3   Conclusions

Access to some foods may be limited for:

• those who are pregnant and not aware of their entitlement (section 6.2.1.i)

• pregnant women who have received information about the teratogenic potential of vitamin A (section 6.2.1.i).

• those from ethnic minority groups who do not understand the literature explaining provisions, or understand how to exchange the tokens (section 6.2.1.i)

• those sent the wrong type of token (section 6.2.1.ii)

• those who cannot store large quantities of liquid milk (section 6.2.1.ii)

• those obliged to exchange their tokens with retailers who fail to conduct a fair exchange (section 6.2.1.ii)

- those who have special medical needs or dietary requirements (section 6.2.1.iii)

- those who have little reason to attend a clinic regularly (section 6.2.1.ii).

Analysis of uptake is difficult because the picture reported by recipients is in many cases difficult to reconcile with WFS/DSS data. There are also several limitations to interpreting the latter. Nevertheless groups vulnerable to low uptake appear to be:

- the 9% of recipients who appear not to exchange their tokens. Reasons for this are unclear.

- a small proportion of beneficiaries who seem not to receive the tokens to which they are entitled (particularly pregnant women and Asian families) (section 6.2.2.i and section 6.2.2.ii).

- older infants whose mothers use the tokens to claim liquid milk rather than formula

- the large proportion of WFS beneficiaries, particularly children, who do not receive vitamins (section 6.2.2.iii). A particularly disturbing finding was that children from households eligible for WFS vitamin supplements are even less likely to take them than children from non-eligible households.

- those children attending day care facilities registered with the WFS (about half) who do not claim their liquid milk entitlement (section 6.2.2.iv). The nutritional consequences of this are, however, unclear.

- a very small number of disabled children claim welfare milk though we have been unable to discover what proportion of those eligible are represented (section 6.2.2.v).

6.3 Intra-household factors which affect whether the intended recipient consumes the product

If the Scheme is to impact upon nutritional risk for the intended recipient, the chain linking access, uptake and consumption must be secure. There are however, some weak links:

- Some tokens are exchanged for products other than milk. In a small 1989 survey 6% of respondents reported exchanging tokens for other food items, and 4% reported exchanging them for non-food items (RSGB, 1989). Given that it is illegal to exchange the tokens for anything other than milk, these data may underestimate the problem.

- Milk or vitamins provided may be consumed by members of the household other than the intended recipient e.g. the elderly or adult men. The extent of this is unknown.

6.4   Estimated effect of WFS on nutritional vulnerabilities of the beneficiaries

Notwithstanding remarks in sections 6.2 and 6.3, we have assumed in subsequent paragraphs that intended recipients consume their full entitlement. In order to estimate the *potential* effect of the Scheme on nutritional risk, the following areas have been examined:

- Nutrient intake

- Dietary practices

- Growth

- Household budgets

- Infant morbidity

6.4.1   Effect on the nutrient intake of beneficiaries
This section will examine the *potential* contribution WFS products make to the nutrient intakes of beneficiary groups. Where intake data are not available we have set the *potential* contribution of products against Dietary Reference Values (DRV). In stressing the word *potential* we reiterate our assumption that those eligible consume the full amount of product to which they are entitled. This clearly is not the case (sections 6.2 and 6.3) but an assessment cannot be made in any other way (section 6.1).

6.4.1.i   *Formula-fed infants aged 0-6 months*
Table 6.8 shows the estimated average requirement (EAR) for energy of infants aged 0-12 months compared to the energy content of formula provided under the Scheme. It shows that until the end of the 4-6 month period, formula entitlement will meet EAR for energy. Complementary foods should then be introduced into the diet (section 4.6.1.i). The nutrient content of infant formula brands currently included in the Scheme is given in Annex 1. This must comply with current legislation (section 4.6.1.i). Annex 1 shows that the nutrient content of different formula brands supplied within the Scheme is very similar.

Table 6.8: Estimated Average Requirement and energy content of formula during infancy

Age (months)	Estimated Average Requirement for energy (kcal per day)	Energy provided by 1 litre formula with energy content of 67 kcal per 100ml (kcal)
0-3	545	
4-6	690	670
7-9	825	
10-12	920	

6.4.1.ii *Infants aged 6-12 months*

Table 6.9 shows the contribution made by welfare foods to DRV for infants aged 6-12 months. The foods are set against DRV as there are no national data, other than the 1986 MAFF survey, on the dietary intakes of children at this stage (Mills & Tyler, 1992). The table indicates that for nutrients identified in section 4.7.2 as being at risk of falling short of DRV, welfare foods potentially provide a large proportion of RNI. Although complementary foods would optimally provide approximately 25-50% of energy intake (Brown *et al*, 1998), at this age the current allocation of formula could provide 73-88% of EAR for energy. The full entitlement of WFS formula might therefore undesirably displace energy provided by the solid food components of a more varied weaning diet, particularly towards the end of the first year of life.

Table 6.9: Proportion of Dietary Reference Values contributed by welfare food allocation for children aged 6-12 months

Nutrients chosen according to their respective importance	DRVs (EAR for energy and RNIs for other nutrients) for children aged 6-12 months*	Nutrient content of daily welfare food allocation			Percent of DRV met by daily Welfare Foods allocation		
		Infant formula 1 litre per day	Whole cow's milk 1 pint per day	Vitamins 5 drops	Infant formula 1 litre per day	Whole cow's milk 1 pint per day	Vitamins 5 drops
Energy kcal	765-920	670	381	0	88-73	41-50	-
Iron mg	7.8	6.6	0.3	0	85	4	-
Vitamin D µg	7	9	0.2	7.15	125	3	102
Zinc mg	5	4.8	2.2	0	97	45	-
Vitamin A µg	350	780	291	214	223	83	61
Vitamin C mg	25	79.4	5.6	21	318	22	84

* (Department of Health, 1991)

Table 6.10: Contribution of cow's milk and infant formula to RNI when given in equal volumes

	% RNI provided by 500ml of infant formula	% RNI provided by 500ml whole cow's milk
Energy	44-37 (EAR)	43-36 (EAR)
Iron	43	3
Vitamin D	63	2
Zinc	49	40
Vitamin A	112	74
Vitamin C	159	20
Copper	50	0
Selenium	89	63

Table 6.9 also gives data for cow's milk and vitamins. Sections 4.6.2.ii and 6.2.2.i showed that cow's milk represents an increasing proportion of the liquid component of children's diets as they grow older. The table indicates that a daily pint of cow's milk would provide a smaller proportion of key nutrients (particularly energy, iron and zinc) than the 1 litre allowance of formula. This is not merely a consequence of discrepancy in the volumes of cow's milk and formula allocated; 500 ml of infant formula per day would still provide considerably greater quantities of iron, vitamin D, vitamin A, vitamin C, copper and selenium (Table 6.10).

6.4.1.iii *Children aged 1-4 years*

Nutrient Intakes
Table 6.11 shows the proportion of nutrient intakes potentially obtainable from welfare foods if children aged 1½-4½ years consumed all they were allocated. Three scenarios are considered:

1. children who receive milk through their family's entitlement to IS or IBJSA, i.e. 1pint of liquid cow's milk per day

2. children whose families are not entitled to IS IBJSA but who receive nursery milk, i.e. 1/3 pint liquid cow's milk per day (five days per week)

3. children who both receive milk through household entitlement to IS or IBJSA and receive nursery milk, i.e. 1.3 pints liquid cow's milk per day.

Table 6.11: Proportion of nutrient intakes which would be contributed if welfare foods were consumed by children aged 1½-4½ years

	Children aged 1½-4½ years whose parents receive benefit: Income Support or Family Credit				Children aged 1½-4½ years whose families do not receive benefit	
	Mean daily intakes from all sources (Gregory *et al*, 1995)	% of intakes coming from 1 pint of whole cow's milk	% intakes coming from 1.3 pints whole cow's milk (i.e. additional nursery milk)	% intakes coming from vitamin drops	Mean daily intakes from all sources (Gregory *et al*, 1995)	% intakes coming from 0.3 pints whole cow's milk
Energy (kcal)	1159	32	41		1134	11
Protein (g)	37	48	63		37	16
Vitamin A (µg)	540	54	70	40	596	16
Thiamine (mg)	0.8	28	37		0.8	9
Riboflavin (mg)	1.2	79	103		1.2	26
Niacin (nic equiv) (mg)	16	29	38		16	9
Vitamin B6 (mg)	1.2	28	37		1.2	9
Vitamin B12 (µg)	2.7	2	3		2.9	0.7
Folate (µg)	133	25	33		131	9
Vitamin C (mg)	42.7	13	17	50	56	3
Vitamin D (µg)	1.9	19	25	375	1.9	3
Vitamin E (mg)	4.4	11	15		4.4	4
Calcium (mg)	625	103	134		643	33
Phosphorus (mg)	731	73	95		747	24
Magnesium (mg)	133	46	60		138	15
Sodium (mg)	1572	11	14		1475	4
Potassium (mg)	1489	53	69		1516	17
Chloride (mg)	2383	23	31		2204	8
Iron (mg)	5.5	5	7		5.6	2
Zinc (mg)	4.4	51	66		4.4	17
Copper (mg)	0.5	Trace	Trace		0.5	Trace
Iodine (µg)	118	84	109		120	28

The table shows 1 pint and 1.3 pints contribute 32% and 41% of the energy intake of children from IS/IBJSA households respectively (scenarios 1 and 2). In the case of children receiving only one third of a pint of nursery milk this would contribute 11% of the energy intake (scenario 3). A pint of milk per day would contribute the entire intake of calcium, 73% of phosphorus, 84% of iodine and 79% of riboflavin but only 9% of vitamin D intake and 5% of iron intake. This is likely to have undesirable consequences for groups of children at risk of iron deficiency (see Section 5.6.1). One third of a pint of milk would contribute less than 10% of the intakes of vitamins C, D and iron of children from families not in receipt of benefit. This further emphasises the importance of vitamin supplements for young children. In this age group they potentially contribute half the intake of vitamins A and C and over three times the intake of vitamin D from food.

While the nursery milk allocation provides about one tenth of the energy intake of children who are not from families in receipt of benefit, the NDNS 1½ – 4½ years showed that a fifth of the calorie intakes of children in this age group came from foods eaten outside the home. The 2.5% of children in this age group who had the highest average energy intake from foods eaten outside the home, consumed on average 75% of their food energy outside the home (Gregory *et al*, 1995). The contribution of nursery milk to the nutrients obtained by children from outside the home cannot be determined as there have been no national surveys of the quality of food provision in day care facilities, nor are there any large-scale studies which compare the diets of children attending day care with those remaining at home (Caroline Walker Trust, 1998).

Milk intakes

Table 6.12A sets consumption data from NDNS 1½-4½ against entitlement under the Scheme. Although younger children generally consumed a greater proportion of their allowance than older ones, as a group they consumed only half their allocation. Amongst those who received the additional allocation of nursery milk an even smaller proportion was consumed. Again, there were major shortfalls in the consumption of vitamin supplements: children consumed only 11% of the potential vitamin C allocation (Table 6.12B). Although increasing the apparent shortfalls in liquid milk consumption would be of dubious value, measures directed towards increasing the uptake of vitamin supplements would probably be beneficial.

Table 6.12: Contribution of welfare foods to food/ supplement intake for children aged 1½-4½ years: A: milk, B: vitamin supplements*

A	Mean daily milk intake of children from households on Income Support (ml)**	% daily allocation of welfare milk (1 pint) volume which is actually consumed	% daily allocation of welfare milk (1.3 pints nursery milk) which is actually consumed
MILK			
Whole milk	244		
Semi-skimmed milk	45		
Total	296	53	41

B	Mean daily nutrient intake from supplements for children from households not in receipt of benefit ***	Mean daily nutrient intake from supplements for children from households in receipt of benefit***	% welfare vitamin allocation which is actually consumed
VITAMINS SUPPLEMENTS			
A (µg RE)	74	60	35
C (mg)	3.5	2.4	11
D (µg)	0.7	0.6	8

* Note that actual consumption of welfare foods has not been measured. Milk and vitamin supplements could have come from any source ** unpublished data from NDNS 1½- 4½ years *** (Gregory *et al*, 1995)

6.4.1.iv *Pregnant and breastfeeding women*

Nutrient intakes

There are no nationally representative data on dietary intakes during pregnancy or lactation. Table 6.13 therefore uses data from a survey which administered a food frequency questionnaire to pregnant women in south-west England. We have used these data because they are recent and distinguish between the intakes of richer and poorer women (identified by a scale of difficulty in affording food – see Section 5.4.1.iii). The table estimates the contribution welfare foods might make to the diets of poorer pregnant women if they consumed all the milk and vitamins for which they were eligible. It shows that if women chose whole milk, the WFS allowance could meet 20% of their mean energy intake, 15% of mean folic acid intake, 3% of mean iron intake but almost three-quarters of mean calcium intake. In reality though it is unlikely that pregnant women consume their full allocation of milk (Table 6.15). From a different perspective the pint of whole milk would contribute 44% of saturated fat intake, or 6.5% of energy intake as saturated fat. This is 4% higher than recommended by COMA (Department of Health, 1991) and over the long term could increase risks to cardiovascular health.

Table 6.13: Proportion of nutrient intakes contributed by welfare foods for pregnant women

Nutrient	Intake of pregnant women with highest level of difficulty in affording food and who were smokers (Rogers *et al*, 1998b)	% nutrients consumed contributed by welfare foods		
		Vitamins (daily dose)	whole milk (1pint)	Semi-skimmed milk (1pint)
Energy (kcal)	1875		20	14
Protein (g)	60.8		29	30
Total fat (g)	72.7		30	12
Saturated fat (g)	30.9		44	18
Vitamin C (mg)	57.6	36	10	10
Vitamin D (µg)	Not available	-	-	-
Folate (µg)	220		15	15
Thiamin (mg)	1.27		18	18
Riboflavin (mg)	1.71		56	59
Niacin (mg)	14.0		33*	35*
Vitamin B6 (mg)	1.68		20	20
Carotene (µg)	1643		7	3
Retinol (µg)	589	36	49	19
Vitamin E (mg)	7.67		7	2
Iron (mg)	9.2		3	3
Zinc (mg)	7.57		30	30
Magnesium (mg)	223		28	28
Potassium (mg)	2446		32	34
Calcium (mg)	930		69	72

* including tryptophan

As data on the intakes of breastfeeding women are very few Table 6.14 examines the contribution of welfare foods to the RNI increment for lactation set by COMA (see Section 4.5.1). The table shows that for folate, zinc and copper the increment was not met by WFS products, though for all other nutrients it was almost completely met by a pint of milk and a vitamin tablet. Fifty per cent of the energy increment was met by 1 pint of milk. There are two vitamin supplements (drops and tablets – see Section 3.1.1) available for breastfeeding women under the Scheme: the tablets contain a higher dose of vitamins A, C and D and therefore better meet the lactation increment.

Table 6.14: Proportion of DRVs met by welfare foods for breastfeeding women

	EAR/RNI increment for lactation*	% of increment met by 1 pint whole milk	% increment met by 1 pint semi-skimmed milk	% increment met by vitamin supplement	
				drops	Tablets
Energy (kcal)	Approx 500	74	52		
Protein (g)	11	163	168		
Thiamin (mg)	0.2	112	112		
Riboflavin (mg)	0.5	190	202		
Niacin (mg)	2	230	245		
Vitamin B12 (µg)	0.5	448	448		
Folate (µg)	60	56	57		
Vitamin C (mg)	30	19	19	70	200
Vitamin A (µg)	350	83	32	61	340
Vitamin D (µg)	10	1	0.5	72	100
Calcium (mg)	550	117	122		7
Phosphorus (mg)	440	121	117		
Magnesium (mg)	50	124	124		
Zinc (mg)	6.0	37	37		
Copper (mg)	0.3	0	0		
Selenium (µg)	15	373	373		

* (Department of Health, 1991)

Table 6.15: Milk intakes during pregnancy (Mathews, 1999, unpublished data)

Milk Intake (pints/day)	Social Class n (%)			
	I & II	IIINM	IIINM, IV, V	No income
<=0.25	24 (9.6)	23 (9.9)	33 (19.1)	13 (18.1)
0.5-0.75	120 (48.0)	98 (42.2)	56 (32.4)	22 (30.6)
>=1.0	106 (42.4)	111 (47.8)	84 (48.6)	37 (51.4)
Total	250	232	173	72

Documented milk intakes

Intakes of milk in the second trimester of pregnancy were taken from a local UK study which employed a food-frequency questionnaire completed at 28 weeks gestation (Table 6.15) (see Mathews *et al*, 1999). Women were asked to indicate which of the following categories most closely corresponded to their daily milk intake: none, a quarter of a pint, half a pint, three-quarters of a pint, 1 pint, or more than one pint.

A higher proportion of women in the lowest two income categories had milk intakes of less than a quarter of a pint per day, but these groups also had proportionally more individuals with high milk intakes. Only a half of women who had no income were drinking volumes equal to or greater than one pint. There was therefore no clear social class trend in milk consumption.

6.4.2   Effect on dietary practices

6.4.2.i   *Does the Scheme discourage breastfeeding?*
The current financial value of 900g (7 litres) of infant formula (£6.23) is at least double the value of seven pints (4 litres) of liquid cow's milk (£2-£3) (section 6.4.4). On this basis some have suggested that the Scheme may be a disincentive to breastfeeding (Hall, 1995; Broadfoot, 1996; UNICEF-UK, 1999a; BMA, 1999; Dodds, 1999). Two studies asked women whether they believed the tokens had discouraged them from breastfeeding. They reported that availability of tokens had not affected women's decisions (McInnes & Tappin, 1996; Wharfe, 1999). When women in a socially deprived area of Glasgow were asked their infant feeding intentions, those eligible for tokens were significantly less likely to want to breastfeed ($p<0.001$). Unfortunately no analysis of confounding factors was undertaken (McInnes & Tappin, 1996).

The 1995 Infant Feeding Survey reported that only 5.7% of mothers who received milk tokens were breastfeeding their babies at the age of 4 months. A further 4.9% were giving breast and "non-human milk" and 89.4% were using only "non-human milk". It is not clear whether this low prevalence of breastfeeding (10.6% at 4 months) is significantly lower than that observed in comparable population groups. For example only 13% of mothers in social class V and 16% of mothers aged 16 or under were still breastfeeding at 4 months (Foster *et al*, 1997).

While there is insufficient evidence to determine whether the Scheme is a disincentive to breastfeeding, the current provisions certainly provide no positive incentive. It is likely that a package of support resources[1] for mothers who choose to breastfeed would be both better accepted and more effective than a pint of milk (section 7.4).

In summary there are few quantitative data to support assertions about the negative impact of the Scheme on breastfeeding, though there is no material incentive to breastfeed. This is a very important area requiring further research.

6.4.2.ii   *Introduction of solids*
Children who consume large quantities of milk may do so at the expense of a more varied diet. Setting aside its many behavioural implications, such a practice may detrimentally affect nutrient intake. The average milk or formula intake of children aged under 2½ studied in NDNS 1½ -4½ years was 2.2 litres per week (Gregory *et al*, 1995). This would imply that welfare foods did not result in an over-dependence on milk, but only because children were not consuming their full allocation (section 6.4.1.iii). The mean figure however conceals wide variation: the 97.5 percentile intake of whole cow's milk among children aged 1½- 2½ years was 5.4 litres per week, considerably more than the recommended maximum of 600ml per day (sections 4.6.1.ii and 4.7.1).

---

[1] Although low income women are least likely to breastfeed, a recent survey has indicated that they are as likely as women from higher income groups to report needing more information about breastfeeding issues (NCT, 1999).

6.4.3 Effect on growth and body composition

Only one randomised controlled trial has examined the provision of milk tokens to pregnant women and children under 5 years. The criteria for selection of participants and the nature of the provisions were different to those of the Scheme. Moreover it is unclear whether the Scheme was suspended locally for the period of study or continued. Tokens for half-a-pint of milk were given to pregnant women and mothers of children under 5 years. No infant formula or vitamins were included. The children's growth was monitored over a five-year period but both the supplemented and control groups showed no significant differences in height or weight gain. Analysis of a sub-group of *vulnerable* [1] children showed similar findings. The milk tokens did not increase milk purchases or milk intake to the extent of the tokens' value. At best they only marginally supplemented the diet and for the most part replaced it (Elwood *et al*, 1981).

Outside the provisions of the Scheme, a few other studies have examined the effect on growth rates of the provision of milk to primary school children (Cook *et al*, 1979; Baker *et al*, 1980; Rona & Chinn, 1989). They showed inconsistent (Cook *et al*, 1979; Rona & Chinn, 1989), non-significant (Rona & Chinn, 1989) or marginally significant (Baker *et al*, 1980) effects on growth. Another study of note is a randomised controlled trial of milk supplementation conducted among adolescent girls in Sheffield (Cadogan *et al*, 1997). A daily supplement of one pint of milk was associated with significant increases of bone mineral density and content, which, if sustained could positively affect peak bone mass.

Although the data generally fail to confirm an effect of milk supplements on growth it would be dangerous to conclude that withdrawing the Scheme would be without effect. Research has generally targeted older children (implicit in the observation that no formula was provided). It would therefore have overlooked any contribution formula provision may have made to early growth in infancy when Welfare Foods provide the entire dietary requirements.

6.4.4 Effect on household budgets and spending

The 1997/8 Family Expenditure Survey showed that the 20% of single parent households with the lowest income (average household size 2.1 persons) spent £28.20 per week on food (ONS, 1998a). The weekly retail cost of 900 grams (which makes up 7 litres) of infant formula provided by the Scheme for a bottle-fed infant averages £6.23. Thus, if low-income households had to purchase infant formula it would account for 22% of their food expenditure. Put another way it would represent 10% of IS payment made to a mother aged 18-24 years. Seven pints (approximately 4 litres) of milk would cost between £2 and £3, approximately half the cost of formula (though volume for volume their costs are similar) and about 5% of the IS received by a young mother with a child.

---

[1] "vulnerable" children were those from families which when the study child was $4\frac{1}{2}$ years had an expenditure on food under £20 per week and 3 or more children, expenditure under £25 per week and 4 or more children or 5 or more children irrespective of the expenditure on food (Elwood *et al*, 1981).

Focus group discussions with welfare food beneficiaries have indicated that they overwhelmingly prefer tokens to cash. They asserted "that way you know the baby gets the milk", or that "you can save it for when you run out of money and at least that way the baby gets the milk" (Wharfe, 1999).

Removal of entitlement to Welfare Foods would clearly have significant effects on the economy of low income households.

6.4.5   Effect on morbidity

Section 6.4.1.i showed that welfare foods make a major contribution to the nutrient intakes of infants, particularly those under 6 months for whom they meet all nutrient requirements. Prior to the development of current infant formula, serious morbidity risks associated with the use of cow's milk or unmodified formula were documented in *"Present day practice in infant feeding"* (1974), which included hyperphosphataemic convulsions, hypernatraemic dehydration and iron deficiency anaemia (DHSS, 1974).

Nutritional rickets is still a matter of serious concern among young children (Department of Health, 1998) and remains evident in the UK (Mughal *et al*, 1999) though it would be preventable if current policy about vitamin D supplementation were implemented. It is also likely that the prevalence would increase among high risk groups if the Scheme were withdrawn.

6.4.6   Conclusions

The conclusions are limited by the available data. Nevertheless it can be concluded that:

- Formula milk supplied by the Scheme provides the entire nutritional requirement for almost all infants under 6 months (section 6.4.1.i).

- Provision of infant formula probably prevents the use of less suitable breastmilk substitutes which would have undesirable health consequences for young children (section 6.4.5).

- A litre of infant formula contributes too great a proportion of DRV for infants aged 6-12 months and may consequently displace complementary foods from the diet (section 6.4.1.ii).

- Children unadvisedly given cow's milk instead of formula in this age group are particularly vulnerable to low iron intakes (sections 6.4.1.i and 6.4.1.ii).

- 1-4 year old children do not consume welfare foods or vitamins in the intended quantities. The provision of nursery milk for children already entitled to allowances with IS and IBJSA exceeds consumption by even greater amounts (section 6.4.1.iii).

- Welfare foods contribute a significant proportion of energy, saturated fat, calcium, riboflavin and vitamin A to the diets of pregnant women but make little contribution to intake of iron and folic acid. Existing welfare foods meet DRV increments for lactation for the majority of nutrients (section 6.4.1.iv). However, the need for such an increment is questionable (section 4.5.1).

- The effects of the scheme on infant feeding decisions about breastfeeding and weaning are difficult to determine and require further research (section 6.4.2).

- In the context of the UK in recent years, milk supplementation has not been proven to have an effect on growth though interventions made were more limited than those made by the WFS and ignored the potentially greater contribution of supplements in infancy (section 6.4.3).

- Free provision of welfare foods releases a significant proportion of the food budget available to households on IS or IBJSA (section 6.4.4).

Chapter 7: Review of other interventions

7.1 Introduction

Our terms of reference required an assessment of *"the <u>contribution</u> of Welfare foods to maintaining adequate nutritional status"*. In chapter 6 we examined the potential contribution of Welfare Foods to dietary intake. The Welfare Food Scheme is only one of many interventions operating in this country and a number of initiatives complementary to the Scheme aim to help maintain and protect the nutritional status of children and pregnant women in the UK. We now review examples of these, together with a brief account of local milk token initiatives which enhance the flexibility of the Scheme.

Local interventions have only been reviewed if they have been formally evaluated. There is a wide range of local food-based projects in the UK including food co-operatives, shopping transport, community cafes, lunch clubs, cookery courses and demonstrations (including the Government initiative "Cooking for Kids"), mobile shops, fruit distribution and Breakfast Clubs (Craig & Dowler, 1997; BMA, 1999). Formal evaluations of these initiatives have not been identified by the Panel. Annex 3 describes evaluations of the WIC Programme in operation in the United States.

7.1.1 Policy context

Interventions cannot be considered without recognition of the policy context within which they operate. The 1999 White Paper *"Saving Lives: Our Healthier Nation"* (TSO, 1999c) is an action plan to tackle poor health which particularly aims to improve the health of the worst off [1]. In addition to creating an enabling environment, policies themselves have been shown to affect practice. Breastfeeding policies supported by media campaigns, implemented in Scotland and Northern Ireland have shown positive effects on breastfeeding prevalence (Kirk, 1980; Bleakney & McErlain, 1996). The forthcoming Regulations on National Nutrition Standards for School Lunches and the Welfare Food Regulations (1996) determine the legal framework within which interventions addressing nutritional vulnerability operate.

---

[1] The 1998 Acheson Inquiry provides the basis for an Our Healthier Nation Action Report entitled "Reducing Health Inequalities" which highlights efforts being made to address inequalities.

7.2　　Interventions other than the Scheme which may alleviate nutritional vulnerability

7.2.1　Professional and peer support

7.2.1.i　*Professional*

- One example is the WHO/UNICEF Baby Friendly Initiative. Although this has been the subject of systematic review (WHO, 1998), there has been no formal evaluation of its impact on outcomes and the prevalence of breastfeeding in the UK. At October 1, 1999 there were 23 Baby Friendly Hospitals in the UK and a further 51 with a certificate of commitment (UNICEF, personal communication). In 1999, a Seven Point Plan was launched to protect, promote and support breastfeeding in community health settings (UNICEF, 1999b). It is unique to the UK but is at a very early stage of development.

- Professional support has been evaluated for the treatment of failure to thrive. Two UK randomised controlled trials of community based interventions have been conducted examining the effect of health visitor support to affected families in Newcastle (Wright *et al*, 1998) and Leeds (Raynor *et al*, 1999). The Newcastle intervention involved specially-trained health visitors, dietitians and community paediatricians. Control children received routine health visitor care (Wright *et al*, 1998). In Leeds children attending a failure to thrive clinic were randomly allocated to routine care or intensive home visiting from a specialist health visitor for 1 year (Raynor *et al*, 1999). Both interventions had positive effects although a significant effect on recovery from FTT was only achieved in Newcastle where anthropometric measurements, on average 2½ years after the initial assessment by the health visitor, showed that a greater proportion of children in the intervention group were nearer their expected weight than in the control group (Wright *et al*, 1998). Non-significant but positive effects on weight gain in infancy were also demonstrated by the study in Leeds in addition to other positive effects including improved feeding behaviour, reductions in the numbers of referrals (to social services and community dietitians), missed appointments and home visits by health visitors (Raynor *et al*, 1999).

7.2.1.ii　*Peer support*

Peer support interventions refer to those where support is provided by trained and knowledgeable persons who are not health professionals but peers working voluntarily within the community (Fairbank *et al*, 1999).

- The Department of Health scheme "Infant Feeding Initiatives" is supporting 20 breastfeeding projects in almost every region of England. Peer support and support group projects form the majority and all will be implemented among groups of women of low socio-economic status. Emphasis has been given to lengthening the duration of breastfeeding in this group in order to address inequalities in health. All projects will be evaluated so that good practice can be disseminated.

- Non-governmental networks of volunteers and professionals operate nationally to support the initiation and duration of breastfeeding. Examples include La Leche League, Breastfeeding Network, National Childbirth Trust and the Association of Breastfeeding Mothers. It is unclear, however, how well mothers from low income families and population groups with traditionally low prevalence of breastfeeding access this network of support.

- The Glasgow Infant Feeding Action Research Project selected two socially deprived areas of the city (Easterhouse and Drumchapel) with the lowest levels of breastfeeding. Easterhouse was offered seven trained peer counsellors resident in that community with recent experience of breastfeeding. Compared to control group mothers who stated an intention to breastfeed at booking, those in the intervention group were significantly more likely to initiate breastfeeding, to be breastfeeding at hospital discharge, and to be breastfeeding at all or exclusively at six weeks (McInnes, 1998).

7.2.2   Parental education

- In 1995-8 the Health Education Authority ran the first national integrated campaign aimed at increasing the average daily intake of folate and folic acid by at least 400µg in women who may become pregnant. The campaign had several objectives which included increasing the awareness of the importance of taking additional folic acid before and until the twelvth week of pregnancy in the general female population (Landon & Thorpe,1998). Research conducted throughout the campaign indicated that spontaneous awareness of folic acid increased from 9% in 1995 to 39% in 1997. Impacts on folic acid supplement use have been suggested in section 5.3.1.ii.

- A randomised controlled trial of parent education intended to improve their children's consumption of dietary iron was conducted in Birmingham inner city communities (Childs et al, 1997). Parental education was provided (orally and in written materials) at key stages (3-4 months, 4-6 months and 9-12 months) by health visitors and focused on the correct use of breastmilk or fortified formula feeds and good weaning diets containing iron rich foods and vitamin C. No effects on diet scores, feeding practices or haemoglobin levels were found. Another UK study noted an improvement in haemoglobin levels following an education intervention, although the difference was small and there was no contemporary control group (James et al, 1989b).

- A study in Aberdeen examined the effect of a nutrition education programme on the knowledge, attitude and dietary intakes of pregnant women. The intervention package was carefully designed to be appropriate to the beneficiary population and showed a positive effect on the knowledge of women in the intervention group compared to controls. However, there was no effect on attitudes which might influence nutrient intake or any effect on dietary intake. The authors concluded achieving dietary change requires more than information alone (Anderson et al, 1995).

In conclusion, evidence suggests that parental education alone has little effect in inducing behavioural change as opposed to increasing knowledge and awareness. It is likely that education would have a better effect if delivered in combination with other measures.

7.2.3   Secondary prevention

Treatment of cases detected by screening ("secondary prevention") has been evaluated in two contexts: iron deficiency anaemia and failure to thrive in childhood. Results in both cases have been disappointing.

- Screening for iron deficiency is not routinely conducted among pre-school children in the UK because:

  - Screening can be regarded as too intrusive and parents may be reluctant to participate. High level of coverage of screening programmes have been reported in areas where community health services are well accepted and communities are informed about the scale of anaemia (James, 1989a, 1989b). However in other contexts, only low levels of coverage have been achieved (James, 1987; Tamhne, 1988).

  - The age offering greatest sensitivity of detection has not been established. The development of iron deficiency anaemia varies according to the age of the child and may be confounded by the velocity of weight gain. This means that children may be anaemic in infancy and recover in their second year or *vice versa* (James, 1995; Hall, 1996).

  - Primary care teams may not have adequate resources to use instruments sufficiently accurate and precise to detect mild cases of iron deficiency anaemia (Hall, 1996).

  - Haemoglobin concentration cut-offs for diagnosing anaemia do not necessarily identify those who are iron deficient or who a pathological cause for their low haemoglobin concentration (Stevens, 1998).

  - Identification of failure to thrive is the main justification for weight monitoring during infancy (Hall, 1996). However, section 5.5.3.i indicated the problems of defining FTT as there is little objective guidance as to what constitutes a normal rate of weight gain. Centile charts for weight are used and problems arise from the assumption that normal growth constitutes tracking along the birth centile:

    - Charts are cross sectional and thus provide only general guidance on individual growth trajectories (Wright *et al*, 1994a) (section 5.2.3).

    - Many children deviate from their earlier centile position ("catch-up" or "catch-down" growth) but it is not always clear when this is pathological (Wright *et al*, 1994a).

- The most commonly used definition of abnormality
  pre-determined centile (usually the third). This is
  attained weight, not growth, and is likely to be bo
  unspecific (Wright *et al*, 1994a).

7.2.4   Food fortification

- In the White Paper *"Saving Lives: Our Healthier Nation"* (TSO, 1999c), the
  Government announced an up-to-date expert scientific review of fluoride and
  health. If the review confirms health benefits of water fluoridation outweigh
  risks, the law will be changed to introduce an obligation on water companies
  to fluoridate where there is strong local support.

- The COMA report: *Folic Acid and the prevention of disease* considered
  "mechanisms including the fortification of foods for the maintenance of
  adequate nutritional status and evaluation of their safety and effectiveness"
  (Department of Health, 2000).

- Mandatory addition of calcium carbonate to white flour and addition of vitamin
  D to spreading fats probably makes a considerable contribution to intakes of
  these nutrients among particular groups of the population. In addition the
  consumption of fortified breakfast cereals and infant or follow-on formulas
  may provide important dietary sources of vitamin D for young children
  (Wharton, 1999). The fortification of chapati flour with vitamin D has also
  been identified as an intervention targeted at children of Asian origin (Aukett
  & Wharton, 1989).

Despite the existence of these programmes there remains strong evidence for the
provision of medicinal vitamin supplements amongst high risk groups such as
young children and women of childbearing age.

7.3   **Local milk token initiatives**

Several local projects in Scotland have developed "milk token initiatives"
involving modification of the Welfare Food Scheme. The Govan Healthy Eating
Project in Glasgow is one example and has the following objectives:

- To encourage parents to acquire milk with the token

- To ensure that the maximum nutritional benefit is received from the token

- To increase substantially the amounts of fresh fruit that pre-school children in
  Govan consume by permitting access to fresh fruit for children under 5 years
  through milk tokens

- To assist in establishing community-led dietary improvement programmes that
  are feasible in operation and affordable to persons living within deprived areas

show that profits made from these tokens can be earned directly by community groups and families involved, adding to the milk token's value and releasing hidden income

- To increase parent participation in self help initiatives in tackling the effects of food poverty (Govan Healthy Eating Project, 1998).

Suppliers of milk under the Welfare Food Scheme are usually shops and other retailers who make a small profit from supplying milk in exchange for tokens. In Govan this profit was used to purchase fresh fruit and vegetables for distribution with milk. Parent volunteers were trained to implement the project though outside funding was required to meet some of the operational costs. It is difficult (though not impossible) for Schemes like this to function effectively within the current legislative framework governing the WFS. However, DH has issued guidelines illustrating how such Schemes can comply with current legal constraints (Annex 4).

7.4   **Conclusions**

- The Welfare Food Scheme is only one of many interventions operating in this country which aim to alleviate nutritional vulnerability. The Scheme's contribution to the nutritional status of beneficiaries cannot be regarded in isolation; indeed any modifications to the current Scheme must endeavour to complement other interventions.

- The wide range of interventions highlighted here appropriately reflects the diverse character of nutritional vulnerability documented in section 6.8.

- In general, behavioural change is more likely to be achieved by provision of educational, material, peer and professional support in combination.

- The effectiveness of the Scheme may be improved by complementing the provision of food with education, training or support, or by adapting the legal framework of the Scheme to make it more flexible for modification at a community level.

Chapter 8: Conclusions

The Welfare Food Scheme retains great potential for improving the health of nutritionally vulnerable pregnant women, mothers and young children but could be improved without additional cost.

8.1   Key conclusions

• The Welfare Food Scheme which began in 1940 (section 2.1), retains great potential for improving the health of pregnant women, mothers and young children who remain nutritionally vulnerable sectors of the population (chapter 2, section 5.1).

• It is increasingly apparent that sub-optimal nutrition at these stages of the life cycle has intergenerational effects which perpetuate deprivation (Acheson, 1998) (section 5.2.5).

• Currently the Scheme is directed principally at families who have very low income (chapter 3). As we have shown, nutritional health outcomes are poorer in such groups than in the more affluent sectors of society (chapter 5).

• One in four children under the age of 5 years lives in a household with sufficiently low income to qualify for benefit (chapter 1). The scale of this problem has implications for the design of a Welfare Food Scheme. If it is to form an effective safety net it must adopt a public health approach rather than cater for the nutritional or specific medical needs of individuals.

• Within the population, pockets of nutritional risk persist (chapter 5). Some of the affected groups are eligible for the benefits of the Scheme (sections 5.2.5, 5.3.1.ii, 5.4.1.iii, 5.5.1.ii, 5.5.2.ii, 5.6.1.iv and 5.6.3.ii) whereas others fall outside (sections 5.4.4.ii, 5.5.2.ii, 5.5.3.iv, 5.6.1.iv, 5.6.2.ii, 5.6.3.ii, 5.7.1.iv and 5.7.2). Despite its effectiveness, the Scheme could undoubtedly be improved without additional cost (sections 8.3, 8.4.2 and 8.5.1).

• The provision of free vitamin supplements offers a simple and potentially effective means of preventing adverse nutritional outcomes, particularly rickets (section 5.6.2.ii). Unfortunately the consumption of vitamin supplements is lowest among beneficiaries of the Scheme (section 6.4.1.iii). Measures which will improve distribution and uptake of vitamin supplements need urgent implementation (section 6.2.1.ii).

- The Scheme offers no material incentive for mothers who choose to breastfeed (section 6.4.2.i), the healthiest option for themselves and their babies (section 6.5.1.i).

- It is nevertheless vital that it continues to meet the whole nutritional requirements of young (0-6 month old) infants whose mothers have chosen to bottle-feed (section 6.4.1.i). The high growth potential and vulnerability to disease in this group places them at particularly high nutritional risk (sections 4.6.1.i and 6.4.5).

- The Scheme has not been reviewed scientifically since its inception. Evaluation is constrained by the lack of an identified group of similar socio-economic status not in receipt of welfare foods as a basis for comparison (chapter 1).

- Any modifications to the current Scheme should complement existing UK programmes and combine practical support with education in order to improve the effectiveness of the Scheme (section 7.4).

- The Panel concluded that consideration should be given to the package of amendments set out in the closing paragraph of this Chapter (section 8.8).

8.2   Pregnant women

The panel concluded that:

- Improving the dietary intake of women of childbearing age has the potential to ensure that nutritional status at conception is adequate to support optimum fetal development (section 5.4.1.ii). Currently welfare foods are provided only after pregnancy is established though there is clear evidence that women are nutritionally vulnerable before conception (sections 4.3.2, 4.8.2 and 5.3.1.ii).

- There are good grounds for targeting pregnant women of low socio-economic status because low intake of many nutrients, particularly micronutrients, is strongly correlated with low social class, low maternal age and low educational attainment (section 5.4.1.iii).

- To a pregnant woman the value of her current welfare foods allowance represents 10% of her income support (IS) allowance, and an even higher proportion of her food budget. Thus, even if the mother does not consume the welfare food herself, resources are released elsewhere in the household budget (section 6.4.4).

- It is likely that enhancing dietary choice, by providing options other than milk alone, would better address the demonstrable inequalities in nutrient intake among women of low socio-economic status (sections 5.4.1.iii and 6.4.1.iv). Local initiatives have demonstrated that choice can be improved at low or negligible cost (section 7.3).

- It is important that pregnant women on the Scheme remain entitled to free vitamin supplements. Without these the existing increment in RNI for pregnancy of vitamin D cannot be met (section 4.4.1). This is especially important for ethnic minority groups for whom extending the supply of free supplements would be an advantage (section 5.4.4.ii).

- The composition of the Department of Health A, C & D vitamin supplement licensed for use in pregnancy requires review (section 3.1.1). The strong social class gradient in vitamin C intake justifies its continued inclusion (section 5.4.1.iii). However, the arguments for retaining vitamin A are less secure; high doses have teratogenic potential in early pregnancy (FAO, 1988) and anecdotal reports suggest its inclusion may deter some women from consuming the combined preparation (section 6.2.1.i).

- Folic acid supplements are not currently provided by the Scheme (section 3.1.1) and uptake of peri-conceptional folic acid supplements amongst population groups who may be Scheme beneficiaries is likely to be poor (section 5.3.1.ii). Free provision of folic acid supplements to beneficiary groups might improve uptake but such a change would need to take account of any changes in policy to improve folate status following the COMA report *Folic acid and the prevention of disease.*

- There is insufficient evidence from a UK perspective to conclude that pregnant women would benefit from medical micronutrient supplementation. Potential for harm as well as benefit needs to be taken into acount.

8.2.1   Pregnant women under 18 years of age
The Panel concluded that:

- The Scheme offers particular potential to address nutritional vulnerability amongst teenage pregnant women, about 90 per cent of whom receive IS (sections 3.1.5.i and 5.8.2.iv). However, welfare food provision varies: women having a first child become entitled only late in pregnancy whereas others receive benefits throughout.

- The younger the pregnant woman, the greater her nutrient requirements (section 4.4.1), and yet the lower her intake is likely to be (sections 5.4.1.iii and 5.8.2.i). In spite of this pregnant women under 18 years have lesser entitlement to welfare foods. Women aged under 16 years who are pregnant or have a child are entitled only if their parents are eligible for IS or IBJSA (sections 3.1.5.i and 5.8.2.ii).

- Improving the uptake of peri-conceptional folic acid supplements by teenage women poses specific additional problems (section 5.3.1.ii).

8.2.2   Information needs

The Panel recommends that further information be obtained on the following points:

- The nutritional status of pregnant women nationally, particularly those of women in ethnic minority and other vulnerable groups.

- Better methods of measuring the relationships between maternal micronutrient *status* and the outcome of pregnancy.

- Reasons for the observed discrepancies in food intake during pregnancy and the effectiveness of strategies aimed to correct them.

- The reasons for low uptake of free vitamin supplements, particularly pre-conceptual folic acid.

8.3   **Mothers**

The Panel concluded that

- Breastfeeding confers health benefits for mothers and babies which are sustained beyond the period of lactation.   Increasing the prevalence of breastfeeding could yield substantial savings in the cost of healthcare (section 5.5.1.i).

- Currently almost all women eligible for the Scheme bottle-feed their babies (sections 6.2.2.i and 5.5.1.ii) and there is no material incentive to breastfeed in the Scheme (6.4.2.i).

- For women who choose to breastfeed the Scheme's provisions need to be better integrated with existing governmental, non-governmental, professional and peer support initiatives (sections 7.2.1 and 7.4).

- There is no evidence that calcium supplements or milk taken during lactation attenuate maternal bone loss or improve long-term skeletal health of the mother. Nor is there evidence that food supplements enhance the mother's ability to lactate (sections 4.5.1 and 5.4.3.i).   Nevertheless, as with all population groups, there could be advantage in enhancing dietary choice.

- The Scheme may need to take account of ethnic and cultural infant feeding decisions. For example, efforts at improving the prevalence of breastfeeding among Asian women may be better directed at increasing duration rather than initiation.(section 5.5.1.ii).

- For women who choose to bottle-feed the cost of formula could constitute approximately 20 per cent of the household food budget (section 6.4.4). It is important for this reason and those given below that this element of the Scheme is retained.

- We see no grounds for changing the current recommendation that lactating women consume the Department of Health A,C & D vitamin tablet. Without this they would not meet the lactation RNI increment set by COMA for vitamin D (section 4.5.1).

8.3.1   Information needs

The Panel recommends that further information be obtained on the following points:

- The reasons for the social inequality in the prevalence of breastfeeding.

- Effectiveness of interventions aimed at increasing breastfeeding in communities where rates are lowest.

- The effect of the provision of infant formula tokens on infant feeding decisions.

- The reasons for low uptake of free vitamin supplements.

- The infant feeding decisions made by mothers of Afro-Caribbean origin.

8.4   **Infants**

8.4.1   Young infants (0-6 months old)

The Panel concluded that:

- Welfare foods provide the entire nutritional requirement of bottle-fed babies at this stage of life (section 6.4.1.i). Infant formula is the only adequate form of breastmilk substitute (section 4.6.1).

- Infancy is a period of very rapid growth led by nutrient intake (section 5.2.2). Undernutrition at this critical period is the precursor of failure to thrive and long-term growth disadvantage (section 5.5.3.iv).

- There is no evidence to suggest that any brand of infant formula provided by the Scheme carries nutritional advantage over another (section 6.4.1.i).

- There is no nutritional basis for including soy formulas in the Scheme. True medical indications are extremely rare and their use carries potential risks (sections 6.2.1.iii.and 5.6.3.ii).

8.4.2   Older infants (6-12 months old)

The Panel concluded that:

- At this stage the continued provision of infant formula significantly reduces risk of vitamin and iron deficiency (sections 5.6.1.iii and 5.6.2.ii).

- The Scheme currently provides 7 litres per week of formula for children in this age group. This is approximately twice the upper boundary of the range of the guidelines (section 4.6.1.ii).

- Low birth weight babies are at increased risk of iron deficiency (section 5.5.4). Extended provision of infant formula rather than cow's milk is therefore particularly important for this group. As infants are entitled to formula only for the first year after birth, those born very early (for example 3 or 4 months prematurely) may receive liquid milk before they attain a corrected age of 1 year post term (section 6.2.1.iii). Given that a significant proportion of children are born in the UK with low birth weight, the Scheme should extend the provision of formula to those babies at the very minimum to 1 year from the expected date of confinement.

- Complementary foods (see Glossary) should be introduced no later than 6 months of age and not before 4 months (section 4.6.1.i). Early introduction is strongly correlated with lower socio-economic status (section 5.5.2.ii). The Scheme has potential to reinforce current recommendations by the timely provision of food products in addition to infant formula (see Annex 3). The cost could be met by reducing the weekly allowance of infant formula to amounts more appropriate.

- Although follow-on formula may be used as part of a progressively diversified diet, at this stage there is no evidence of benefit over the standard infant formulas provided by the Scheme (section 5.6.1.iii).

- The current Scheme allows a mother to choose between liquid cow's milk and infant formula regardless of her infant's age (section 3.1.1). Early introduction of liquid cow's milk is associated with low socio-economic status (sections 5.4.2.iv and 6.2.2.i). The Scheme could be adapted to discourage this practice and thereby reduce the risk of subsequent iron and vitamin D deficiency (sections 5.6.1.iv and 5.6.2.ii). Such a change would require that age-restrictions be placed on the type of token. Equally as important-the system by which mothers access infant formula would need improvement (section 6.2.1.ii).

- COMA recommends supplementation with vitamins A and D for breastfed infants over 6 months and those who consume less than 500ml of infant formula per day (section 4.6.1.ii). The provision of free vitamin supplements under the Welfare Food Scheme provides a safety net for children who may have low intake (for example in association with failure to thrive), increased requirements (for example during infections), or vulnerability to low vitamin D status by virtue of their ethnic origin (section 5.6.2.ii).

- National data continue to show that uptake of vitamins falls far short of the recommended universal use (sections 5.4.4.ii and 5.6.2.ii), particularly amongst low income families (section 6.4.1.iii). Distribution of supplements is currently only through child health clinics and appears to be a significant barrier to uptake (section 6.2.1.ii). This needs to be urgently addressed and consideration given to broadening entitlement to groups other than current beneficiaries of the Scheme, particularly children from ethnic minority families.

8.4.3   Information needs
The Panel recommends that further information be obtained on the following points:

- The reasons why some mothers choose to claim cow's milk rather than infant formula for their infants (section 6.2.2.i).

- The effect of the provision of tokens for age appropriate complementary foods at the expense of infant formula on infant feeding practices.

- Factors which determine the range and quality of complementary foods given to children in low income families.

- The dietary intakes and nutritional status of children aged 6-18 months, particularly those in vulnerable groups.

- The reasons for low uptake of free vitamin supplements.

8.5   **Young children**

8.5.1   Children from households in receipt of benefit (IS & IBJSA)
The Panel concluded that:

- Products supplied under the Scheme continue to meet a large proportion of the child's dietary requirements even after the first birthday (section 6.4.1.iii). However, volume for volume, infant formula is a richer source of iron, vitamin D and vitamin C than cow's milk (section 6.4.1.ii).

- UK-based controlled trials have demonstrated that providing infant formula rather than cow's milk beyond the first birthday significantly reduces the prevalence of iron deficiency anaemia (section 5.6.1.iii). For children up to 2 years of age replacing the current allowance of liquid cow's milk (1 pint per day) with the equivalent volume of infant formula would both improve nutrient intake and reduce the risk of iron deficiency at no additional cost. We conclude that this alternative should be offered together with appropriate advice on the quality of complementary feeding.

- The Scheme does not address the very high risk of dental caries amongst children in this sector of the population (section 5.6.3.ii). However, the Panel strongly endorse preventive action through the fluoridation of water supplies (section 7.2.4) and reinforce advice in *Weaning and the Weaning Diet* that infant formula should be given by cup rather than bottle at the latest by 1 year of age.

8.5.2   Children attending registered daycare facilities
The Panel concluded that:

- Children only access this aspect of the Scheme if the facility which they attend is registered with the Scheme (section 6.2.2.iv) and there is no evidence that they are any more vulnerable nutritionally than those who are at home or attending unregistered facilities (section 6.4.1.iii).

- If children satisfying criteria for inclusion in the Welfare Food Scheme attend registered facilities there is a risk of duplicating milk allocations, such that they may receive as much as 1.3 pints of liquid cow's milk per day. This may prove detrimental to acceptance of a more varied diet (section 6.4.2.ii).

8.5.3   Vitamins for young children
The Panel concluded that:

- In keeping with *Weaning and the Weaning Diet,* children not consuming infant formula or follow-on formula should continue to consume a vitamin supplement until the age of 5 years. Health professionals may need to be better informed of this recommendation.

- As in the case of pregnant women and infants, Scheme beneficiaries appear less likely to accept conform to this recommendation than more affluent groups (section 6.4.1.iii). Again, improved access to vitamin supplements is urgently required (section 6.2.1.ii).

8.5.4   Information needs
The Panel recommends that further information be obtained on the following points:

- The quality and nature of food provision in day care facilities as children obtain a significant proportion of their dietary energy from sources outside the home (section 6.4.1.iii).

- Factors which lead to the inappropriately early introduction of solid foods in the diets of young infants (section 4.6.2.i.).

- Further strategies aimed at reducing iron deficiency anaemia particularly in ethnic minority groups.

- Reasons for the low uptake of vitamin supplements.

8.6   **School age children and adolescents**
The Panel concluded that:

- Currently the Welfare Food Scheme does not target school age children.

- Significant proportions of adolescent girls have intakes of certain minerals (such as iron, magnesium and calcium) which fall short of LRNI (sections 4.8.2 and 5.7.2). These findings may have implications for attainment of peak bone mass in adulthood.

- A proportion of these girls will become mothers whose nutritional status at conception may already be compromised.

- Missing breakfast was widespread among school children and was even more prevalent among children coming from households in receipt of benefit (section 5.7.2). The Panel endorse initiatives such as Breakfast Clubs which aim to increase the number of children having breakfast (section 7.1).

- School age children are increasingly vulnerable to fatness (section 0). Both diet and lack of exercise play a part. The Panel endorsed population-based initiatives such as the Regulations on National Nutritional Standards for School Lunches which aim to improve the quality of dietary intake among school children (sections 4.8.1 and 7.1).

8.6.1   Information needs

The Panel recommends that further information be obtained on the following points:

- Effective interventions to prevent obesity in children.

- Long-term consequences of low mineral intake amongst adolescents.

- Eating patterns of school age children, particularly correlations with socio-economic status.

8.7   Children with special clinical and dietary needs

The Panel concluded that:

- The current Scheme should continue to be viewed as a public health rather than a medical intervention.

- The very small number of children receiving WFS benefits by virtue of inability to attend school suffer from such a diverse range of medical conditions (section 6.2.2.v) that no universal nutritional justification for providing milk can be made.

- Poor families may have difficulty in meeting the higher cost of food for children with increased nutritional requirements where items cannot be prescribed. Although some may be able to obtain the Disability Living

117

Allowance the application procedure does not include assessment sufficient to identify special nutritional needs (section 6.2.1.iii).

8.8   Package of suggested amendments to the Scheme

Pregnant women
- Choices other than milk should be offered to address dietary inequalities more effectively.

- The composition of vitamin supplements should be reviewed. A supplement providing vitamins D, C and folic acid but omitting A would be preferable to the current preparation.

- The Scheme should ensure that pregnant women of all ages have equitable access to Welfare Foods.

Mothers
- An incentive to breastfeed should be considered, replacing the allowance of cow's milk.

Infants
- Liquid cow's milk should not be provided for infants under 12 months of age.

- At 6 months of age the allowance of infant formula should halve in favour of providing tokens to purchase complementary foods.

- Low birth weight babies should be entitled to receive formula until at least 1 year from the expected date of delivery, not the date of birth.

Young children
- Mothers should be offered an equal volume of infant formula as an alternative to cow's milk until the child is at least 18 months of age.

- Consideration should be given to extending the provision of free vitamin supplements to groups who are not beneficiaries of the current Scheme, particularly children from ethnic minority groups.

Nursery milk
- Provision should take account of the child's milk entitlement at home so that total daily milk intake is not excessive to the detriment of a more varied weaning diet.

Children with special needs
- The Disability Living Allowance should take account of special nutritional needs of children in low income families who are affected by medical conditions. This should replace cow's milk and ensure that provision is more appropriate to individual needs.

Annex 1: Nutrient composition of infant formula available on the Scheme

per 100ml made up feed	Cow and Gate Premium	Farley's First	Milupa Aptamil First	SMA Gold	Cow and Gate Plus	Farley's Second	Milupa Milumil	Milupa Aptamil Extra	SMA White
Energy (kcal)	67	68	67	67	67	66	67	67	67
Protein (g)	1.4	1.45	1.5	1.5	1.7	1.7	1.9	1.9	1.6
Whey	0.8	0.89	0.9	60 } ratio	0.3	20 } ratio	0.4	0.4	20 } ratio
Casein	0.6	0.56	0.6	40 } ratio	1.4	80 } ratio	1.5	1.5	80 } ratio
Carbohydrate (g)	7.5	6.96	7.2	7.2	7.3	8.3	8.1	8.1	7
Sugars (lactose) (g)	7.5	6.96	7.2	7.2	7.2	2.8	6.1	8.1	7
Fat (g)	3.5	3.62	3.6	3.6	3.4	2.9	3.1	3.7	3.6
Vitamin A (µg) RE	84	100	60	75	84	80	63	63	75
Vitamin D (µg)	1.4	1.0	1	1.1	1.4	1.0	1.1	1.1	1.1
Vitamin E (mg)	1.1	0.48	0.6	0.74	1.1	0.47	0.6	0.6	0.74
Vitamin K (µg)	5	2.7	3	6.7	5	2.9	3.2	3.2	6.7
Thiamin (µg)	40	42	40	100	40	39	40	40	100
Riboflavin (µg)	120	55	120	150	140	53	60	80	150
Niacin equiv (µg)	750	690	1500	900	750	660	1300	1300	500
Vitamin B6 (µg)	40	35	40	60	40	33	40	40	60
Vitamin B12 (µg)	0.22	0.34	0.2	0.2	0.15	0.13	0.2	0.2	0.2
Total folate (µg)	10	3.4	10	8	10	3.4	11	11	8
Pantothenic acid (µg)	300	280	400	300	300	220	400	400	300
Biotin (µg)	1.5	1.0	1.0	2	1.5	1.1	1.0	1.0	2
Vitamin C (mg)	8	6.9	8	9	8	6	8	8	9
Sodium (mg)	19	17	26	16	24	19	25	20	22
Potassium (mg)	68	57	82	70	90	86	97	88	80
Chloride (mg)	43	40	51	43	56	47	63	63	55
Calcium (mg)	54	39	60	46	80	55	76	84	56
Phosphorus (mg)	27	27	38	33	48	46	46	56	44
Magnesium (mg)	5	5.2	5.2	6.4	5.7	5.5	8	8	5.3
Iron (mg)	0.5	0.65	0.7	0.8	0.5	0.70	0.7	0.7	0.8
Copper (µg)	40	42	40	33	40	40	30	30	33
Zinc (mg)	0.5	0.34	0.5	0.6	0.5	0.33	0.5	0.5	0.6
Taurine (mg)	5.3	5.0	7.0	3.76	5.3	5.0	6.0	8.0	3.76
Iodine (µg)	10	4.5	10	10	10	10	9.1	9.1	10

Annex 2: Benefit entitlement

Three types of benefit provide access to the Welfare Foods Scheme in Great Britain:

- Income Support

- Job Seekers Allowance (income-based)

- Family Credit.

Full details can be obtained at www.dss.gov.uk/ba. A short summary relevant to persons covered by the Panel's Terms of Reference follows:

Income Support:

Eligibility: People over 16 who are unable to work and whose income falls below a minimum level set by Parliament. They must fall into one or more of the following categories:

- lone parent

- unable to work by virtue of illness or disability

- caring for a disabled or ill family member

- pregnant, within 11 weeks of expected confinement

- refugee

Rates of support (1999):

- Single person £30.95 (aged 16-17) to £51.40 (aged 25+) per week

- Couple £61.35 (both aged 16-17) to £80.65 (aged 18+)

- Lone parent – rates as for single person but highest rate from aged 18+ rather than 25+

- Dependent children – between £20.20 (under 11 years) to £30.95 (16-18 years) per child, per week

- Additional premiums between £13.90 and £79.50 are payable to those whose expenses are higher than normal.

Associated Welfare Food Scheme benefit:

The following foods are provided free of charge to:

- Pregnant women: 1 pint of whole or semi-skimmed (not skimmed) milk per day, plus Department of Health vitamin supplement

- Children under 1 year of age: 1 pint of whole or semi-skimmed milk per day (breastfeeding mothers) or 900 grams of infant formula per week plus Department of Health vitamin supplement

- Young children (1-5 years of age): 1 pint of whole or semi-skimmed milk per day plus Department of Health vitamin supplement.

Jobseeker's Allowance (income based)

Income Based Jobseeker's Allowance (IBJSA) should be distinguished from Contribution Based Jobseeker's Allowance which does not provide access to Welfare Foods Scheme benefits.

Eligibility: Jobseeker's Allowance is paid for unemployed people (or those working on average less than 16 hours a week), if they are available for work, are actively seeking employment, and are capable of work. 16 and 17 year olds are only eligible if they are classed as being in a vulnerable group. This could be someone:

- Who is forced to live away from their parents or carers; or

- Couples with children; or

- Those being released from custody or local authority care

and:

- If they will suffer severe hardship if JSA is not paid.

Rates of support (1999):
- Single person £30.95 (aged 16-17) to £51.40 (aged 25+) per week

- Couple £30.95 (both aged 16-17) to £80.65 (aged 18+)

- Dependent children – between £20.20 (under 11 years) to £30.95 (16-18 years) per child, per week.

- Additional premiums between £13.90 and £79.50 are payable to those whose expenses are higher than normal.

Associated Welfare Food Scheme benefit:

The following foods are provided free of charge to:

- Pregnant women: 1 pint of whole or semi-skimmed (not skimmed) milk per day, plus Department of Health vitamin supplement

- Children under 1 year of age: 1 pint of whole or semi-skimmed milk per day (breastfeeding mothers) plus Department of Health vitamin supplement or 900 grams of infant formula per week plus Department of Health vitamin supplement

- Young children (1-5 years of age): 1 pint of whole or semi-skimmed milk per day plus Department of Health vitamin supplement.

Family Credit

From 5 October 1999 this was replaced with the Working Families' Tax Credit (WFTC). Entitlement to Welfare Food Scheme benefits was extended to WFTC recipients who are receiving full WFTC or credit reduced by £70 or less.

Entitlement: Families where at least one partner works 16 hours or more a week and who have one or more children aged under 16 (or under 19 if in full-time education). Family credit entitlement is based on income.

Rates (1999):

- Adult credit (one payable per family): £49.80

- 30 hour credit (one payable per family) if recipient or partner work more than 30 hours a week: £11.05

- Child credits (for each child): £15.15 (0-11 years) to £25.95 (16- 19 years)

If the family's net income is less than £80.65 per week the maximum level of family credit is paid (adult + child + 30hour (if applicable) credits). If the net income exceeds £80.65, seventy pence of every excess £1 is deducted from the maximum family credit.

Associated Welfare Food Scheme benefit:

The following foods are available at a cost of £3.90 (from October, 1999):

Children under 1 year of age: 900 grams of infant formula per week.

Annex 3: The WIC programme in the United States

The Special Supplemental Food Programme for Women, Infants and Children (WIC) was set up in 1972. It aims to improve the nutrition and health status of low income, nutritionally at risk pregnant, breastfeeding and postpartum women, and pre-school children by providing supplemental food, nutrition education and co-ordinated health care (BMA, 1999). Federal funds are allocated to State Departments of Health and local private and public health service providers implement the Programme.

Criteria for eligibility are based on:

- income below 185% of the "poverty line" based on the cost of a nutritionally adequate diet (IOM, 1996)

- assessment of nutritional risk (Committee of Scientific Evaluation of WIC nutrition risk criteria, 1996). Nutritional risk is assessed from biochemical and anthropometric measurements, together with prevalence of nutrition-related medical conditions, high risk pregnancies and dietary deficiencies. Examples include prevalence of anaemia, underweight, low birth weight and teenage pregnancy (Owen & Owen, 1997)

- identified nutritional risks are then subjected to a 7 layer eligibility priority system (Owen & Owen, 1997). The group with highest priority are "pregnant and lactating women and infants at nutritional risk as demonstrated by anthropometric or biochemical assessment or by other documented nutritionally related medical condition" (Owen & Owen, 1997).

Programme inputs

75% of WIC funds are spent on supplemental foods and local WIC agencies must spend a sixth of their administrative funds on nutrition education (Owen & Owen, 1997). Food vouchers are provided for:

- Iron-fortified formula for artificially-fed infants up to 12 months of age

- iron-fortified cereal and vitamin C fortified juice for infants 6-12 months

- milk, adult (iron-fortified) cereal, eggs, vitamin C fortified or citrus juice, cheese and dried beans for children aged 1-5 years (BMA, 1999)

- milk, cheese, cereal (iron-fortified), eggs, vitamin C fortified or citrus juice and dried beans for pregnant and lactating women.

In 1991, breastfeeding promotion in WIC programmes became federally mandated and therefore breastfeeding education and peer-counsellors became a more integral part of the programme (Fairbank *et al*, 1999).

Effect of the Programme

In accordance with our comments on the UK Welfare Food Scheme (chapter 1), the absence of an adequate control group also presents an obstacle to evaluation. In the case of the WIC programme, however, not all those eligible are enrolled – either on account of federal resource limitations or because individuals may decline participation (Poppendieck, 1997). Such groups have sometimes been used as controls in some evaluations of the programme.

The following effects of the Scheme have been noted in local studies:

- Reduction in the prevalence of low birth weight through the provision of pre-natal care, "Medicaid case management services" and supplemental food (e.g. Buescher *et al*, 1993)

- Positive effects on the growth rates of infants (e.g. Heimendinger *et al*, 1984)

- WIC programme foods contributed almost a quarter of the RDA for vitamins A, E and C among pre-school children. In addition 17% of iron and 11% of zinc intakes were contributed, amounting to 1.7 and 1.1 mg/day respectively (Rose *et al*, 1997)

- Increased incidence and prevalence of breastfeeding has been observed, particularly when interventions were combined (Fairbank *et al*, 1999). The commonest were: breastfeeding education classes combined with incentives to participate, promotional materials (e.g. videos), and peer-counselling

- The prevalence of childhood anaemia declined by more than 5% among low income families between 1980-91. Nevertheless frequency remained above that of the general population (Yip *et al*, 1992) and also declined in wealthier groups suggesting secular change (Yip *et al*, 1987a). These trends have been partly attributed to the provisions of the WIC programme (Yip *et al*, 1987b).

Annex 4: Guidelines for Milk Token Initiatives

Background to Milk Token Initiative

The Milk Token Initiative was initially designed and launched in Govan, Glasgow as a "provide and promote" strategy to help ensure that Welfare Food beneficiaries received their full milk entitlement and to encourage and facilitate the consumption of fresh fruit and vegetables. At the same time it was realised that there was a need to offer positive messages about fresh fruit consumption and examine practical ways of interpreting mainstream health education messages about healthy eating.

Milk Tokens

If a family on Income Support or Income Based Jobseeker's Allowance includes:

* a pregnant woman; or

* a child under five

they are entitled to a fresh milk token which can be exchanged for:

* four litres or seven pints of cow's milk a week.

If a child is breast-fed the mother can drink the milk herself. Alternatively, bottle-fed babies aged under one year can receive 900 grammes of dried baby milk by obtaining a dried milk token instead.

A Milk Token Initiative

A community group can apply to register with the Welfare Food Reimbursement Unit (WFRU) as an approved liquid milk supplier. WFRU will reimburse the group for milk supplied.

* The difference between the reimbursement price and the actual cost of milk is the surplus or **profit**.

* Operating as a Milk Co-operative (where all profit is returned to members) the **profit** can be returned to families as a **healthy dividend** .

* The **healthy dividend** is a bag of fruit and vegetables.

- A dividend bag of fruit and veg worth £1 wholesale may be worth double this when set against local retail prices.

How does this work?

A group will set up a sale and milk token redemption point at a suitable location which is open at specific times. Community groups generally choose to operate 2 days a week at a point such as a nursery. When a parent hands in a token they will receive their dividend bag and half of their milk. Suitable records should be kept to enable the customer to collect the rest of their milk later in the week.

Benefits

- Added value adds incentive to redeem token for milk.

- Guaranteed redemption of token if you follow the guidance in this leaflet.

- Children acquire their taste preferences by the age of 5. This initiative offers an opportunity to influence their tastes from an early age.

- Freshest possible milk with highest possible **nutritional content**.

- The 'shop-keepers profit' on a token is returned to the family thereby **maximising income**.

- Families can **experiment** with fruit etc. at no extra cost.

- Families can become more aware of entitlements.

- Opportunity for parents to volunteer.

How can a Community Group register with WFRU

Any community group who wishes to set up a Milk Token Initiative must register with the WFRU which is operated on behalf of the Health Departments of Great Britain.

- **Meeting the Registration Requirements**

To be eligible for registration as a 'supplier', you **must** sell milk to cash customers. You must:

- be a "retailer" – that is you must sell milk at a price which attracts sales;

- be able to show that you sell a reasonable amount of milk to cash customers;

   There is no definition of "reasonable" but remember you can return any profit you make from cash sales as a healthy dividend to your customers.

- supply 7 pints of milk, or 8 half-litres which is the equivalent of 4 litres of milk, to customers exchanging milk tokens;

- have a constitution (only properly constituted groups can apply);

- have a bank account (payments from WFRU will be by Bankers' Automated Clearing System (BACS)).

The Department of Health, as a safeguard against abuses, will also require to see Annual Accounts.

- **Getting registered with WFRU as a 'supplier'**

To get registered you need to:

- Obtain a supplier registration pack from WFRU. Tel. 01536 408008.

- **Completing the registration form:-**

MTI's must register as "MTI" under the category "other" as the type of business on this form and enclose a copy of your group's constitution that outlines your charitable aims and objectives. Once you've been allocated a reference number WFRU will send you a claim form and envelopes to redeem your tokens.

- **Claiming payment**

WFRU makes payments based on the "Approved Price" for milk i.e. the lowest price that you charge for a pint (or half-litre if you supply milk only in metric measures) of pasteurised whole milk during the course of the week in which the milk is supplied in exchange for a token.

Payments

WFRU will then pay you seven times the approved price per pint less a discount which is normally 9% (see *Stage Four* below).

Payments are normally received within 2 weeks by BACS. You will receive a remittance advice by post together with a form to enable you to make your next claim.

How your approved price changes

As the price you charge to the customer changes so too does the approved price – it is always the lowest price that was charged. If a supplier has several outlets selling milk and claims for any tokens received together, the approved price is the lowest price charged in that week at any of the supplier's outlets.

- **How to set your cash price**

Stage One

Survey local shops and establish their selling price for milk.

Decide what price you want to sell milk for. This **must** be a price that will attract cash sales.

Stage Two

Calculate your approved price for registration with WFRU. If you sell milk in ½ litres or pints, the approved price will be your selling price per ½ litre or per pint. But if, for example, you only sell milk in 2 litres jugs, your approved price will be the 2 litre price, divided by 4. If you sell milk only in 1 litre packs, your approved price will be the 1 litre price divided by 2.

Stage Three

The difference between the amount you pay for your milk and the price you are reimbursed by WFRU is the "shopkeepers profit". You can return this profit as a "healthy dividend" but remember to allow for overheads such as wastage and breakage.

Stage Four

WFRU normally deduct a 9% discount from your "approved price" unless you have a high proportion of "token sales" in comparison to cash sales. Reduced discounts may apply if your welfare milk sales amount to more than 7.5% of your total retail sales. Ask WFRU for a Special Discount Application Form.

A new project must show figures for milk supplied under the MTI for the 13 weeks prior to application. Older projects must show one year's books.

An accountant must sign the declaration on the Special Discount Application Form.

What happens to the profits of the cash-sold milk?

You may also return this profit as a healthy dividend to these customers.

References

Abraham R, Campbell-Brown M, North W, McFadyen R, (1987), Diets of Asian pregnant women in Harrow: iron and vitamins. *Hum Nutr: Appl Nutr* **41 A:** 164-173

Acheson, D, (1998), *Independent Inquiry into Inequalities in Health.* London: TSO.

Alberman E & Noble J, (1999), Commentary: food should be fortified with folic acid. *BMJ* **319**: 93

Alfaham M, Woodhead S, Pask G, Davies D, (1995), Vitamin D deficiency: a concern in pregnant Asian women. *Br J Nutr* **73**: 881-887

Allen L, (1997), Pregnancy and Iron Deficiency: Unresolved Issues. *Nutr Rev* **55**: 91–101

Allen L, (1998), Women's dietary calcium requirements are not increased by pregnancy or lactation. *Am J Clin Nutr* **67**: 591-592

American Academy of Pediatrics Committee on Nutrition, (1991), The use of fruit juice in the diets of young children. *AAP News* **7**: 11

Anderson A & Hunt K, (1992), Who are the healthy eaters? Eating patterns and health promotion in the west of Scotland. *Health Education Journal* **51**: 3-10

Anderson A & Campbell D, (1995), The influence of dietary advice on nutrient intake during pregnancy. *Br J Nutr* **15**: 105-177

Audit Commission, (1998), *First class delivery: a national survey of women's views of maternity care.* London: Audit Commission.

Aukett M, Parks Y, Scott P, Wharton B, (1986), Treatment with iron increases weight gain and psychomotor development. *Arch Dis Child* **61**: 849-857

Aukett A & Wharton B, (1989), *Nutrition of Asian children: infants and toddlers in Ethnic factors in health and disease.* ed. Cruickshank JK & Beevers DG. London: Butterworth-Heinemann Ltd.

Baker I, Elwood P, Hughes J, Jones M, Moore F, Sweetnam P, (1980), A randomised controlled trial of the effects of the provision of free school milk on the growth of children. *Epidemiol Comm Hlth* **34**: 31-34.

Baker D, Taylor H & the ALSPAC study team, (1997), The relationship between condition-specific morbidity, social support and material deprivation in pregnancy and early motherhood. *Soc Sci Med* **9**: 1325-1336

Ball T & Wright A, (1999), Health care costs of formula feeding in the first year of life. *Pediatrics* **103**: 870-876

Barker D, (1992), *Fetal and Infant origins of Adult disease.* London: BMJ Publishing.

Batchelor J, (1996), Has recognition of failure to thrive changed? *Child: care, health and development* **22**: 235-240

Bauchner H, Leventhal JM, Shapiro ED, (1986), Studies of breastfeeding and infections. How good is the evidence? *JAMA* **256**: 887-990

Black M, Dubowitz H, Hutcheson J, Berenson-Howard J, Starr R, (1995), A randomised clinical trial of home intervention for children with failure to thrive. *Pediatrics* **95**: 807-814

Black A, Wiles S, Paul A, (1986), The nutrient intakes of pregnant and lactating mother of good socio-economic status in Cambridge, UK: some implications for recommended daily allowances of minor nutrients. *Br J Nutr* **56**: 59-72

BMA, (1999), *Growing up in Britain.* London: British Medical Association.

Boddy J & Skuse D, (1994), Annotation: The Process of parenting in Failure to Thrive. *J Child Psychol Psychiat* **35**: 401-424

Booth I & Aukett M, (1997), Iron deficiency anaemia in infancy and early childhood. *Arch Dis Child* **76**: 549-554

Boyle PJ, Gatrell A, Duke-Williams O, (1999), The effect on morbidity of variability in deprivation and population stability in England and Wales : an investigation at small area level. *Soc Sci Med* **49**: 791-799

BPA, (1994), Is breastfeeding beneficial in the UK? *Arch Dis Child* **71**: 376-380

Bremer H, Brooke O, Orzalesi M, Putet G, Raiha N, Senterre J, Shaw J, Wharton B, (1987), Nutrition and feeding of preterm infants. *Acta Paed Scand* **supp 336**

Bristow A, Qureshi S, Rona RJ, Chinn S, (1997) The use of nutritional supplements by 4-12 year olds in England and Scotland. *Eur J Clin Nutr* **51**: 366-69

British Dental Association, British Society of Paediatric Dentistry & the British Association for the Study of Community Dentistry, (1997), Fluoride supplement dosage. *BDJ* **182**: 6-7

British Fluoridation Society, (1997), *Dental health inequalities in the United Kingdom.* November 2nd edition. London: British Fluoridation Society.

Broadfoot M, (1996), Milk Tokens – time to move on? *New Generation Digest: December.*

Brooke OG, Brown IRF, Bone CDM, Carter ND, Cleeve HJW, Maxwell JD, Robinson VP, Winder SM, (1980), Vitamin D supplements in pregnant Asian women: effects on calcium status and fetal growth. *BMJ* **280**:751-754

Brundtland G, Liestol K, Walloe L, (1980), Height, weight and menarcheal age of Oslo school children during the last 60 years. *Ann Hum Biol* **7**: 307-322

Buescher P, Larson L, Nelson M, Lenihan A, (1993), Prenatal WIC participation can reduce low birth weight and newborn medical costs: a cost benefit analysis of WIC participation in North Carolina. *J Am Diet Assoc* **93**: 163-166

Bush H, Williams R, Sharma S, Cruickshank K, (1997), *Opportunities for and barriers to good nutritional health in minority ethnic groups*. London : Health Education Authority.

Cade J, (1992), Diets of adults living in houses in multiple occupation. *Eur J Clin Nutr* **46**: 795-801

Caraher M, Dixon P, Lang T, Carr-Hill R, (1998), Access to healthy foods: part 1 Barriers to accessing healthy foods: differentials by gender, social class and mode of transport. *Health Education Journal* **57**: 191-201.

Caraher M, Dixon P, Lang T, Carr-Hill R, (1999), The state of cooking in England: the relationship of cooking skills to food choice. *British Food Journal* **101**: 590-609

Caroline Walker Trust, (1998), *Eating well for under 5s in child care. Practical and Nutritional Guidelines*. London: Caroline Walker Trust.

Chappell L, Seed P, Briley A, Kelly F, Lee R, Hunt B, Parmar K, Bewley S, Shennan A, Steer P, Poston L, (1999), Effect of antioxidant on the occurrence of pre-eclampsia in women at increased risk : a randomised trial. *Lancet* **354**: 810-815

Childs F, Aukett A, Darbyshire P, Ilett S, Livera L, (1997), Dietary education and iron deficiency anaemia in the inner city. *Arch Dis Child* **76**: 144-147

Chinn S, (1995), Monitoring the growth of children: conclusions from a long-term study. *Int J Epidimiol* **24**: 575-578

Chinn S, Hughes J, Rona R, (1998), Trends in growth and obesity in ethnic groups in Britain. *Arch Dis Child* **78**: 513-517

Clements M, Mitchell E, Wright S, Esmail A, Jones DR, Ford RPK, (1997), Influences on breastfeeding in southeast England. *Acta Paediatr* **86**: 51-56

Cole TJ, (1994), Do growth chart centiles need a facelift? *BMJ* **308**: 641-642

Cole TJ, Freeman JV, Preece MA, (1998), British 1990 growth reference centiles for weight, height, body mass index and head circumference fitted by maximum penalised likelihood. *Stat Med* **17**: 407-429

Committee on Scientific evaluation of WIC Nutrition Risk Criteria, Food and Nutrition Board, Institute of Medicine, National Academy of Sciences, (1996), Summary of WIC nutrition risk criteria: a scientific assessment. *J Am Diet Assoc* **96**: 925-930

Cook J, Irwig L, Chinn S, Altman D, du Florey C, (1979), The influence of availability of free school milk on the height of children in England and Scotland. *J Epid Comm Health* **33**: 171-176

Corbett S, Drewett R, Wright C, (1996), Does a fall down a centile chart matter? The growth and developmental sequelae of mild failure to thrive. *Acta Paediatr* **85**, 1278-1283

Craig G & Dowler E, (1997), Poverty, Hunger and UK State in *First World Hunger* ed. Riches G ed. Cambridge: Cambridge University Press.

Daly A, MacDonald A, Aukett A, Williams J, Wolf A, Davidson J, Booth I, (1996), Prevention of anaemia in inner city toddlers by an iron supplemented cow's milk formula. *Arch Dis Child* **75**: 9-16

de Andraca I, Castillo M, Walter T, (1997), Psychomotor Development and Behaviour in Iron-deficient Anaemic Infants. *Nutrition Reviews* **55**: 125-132

de Groot L, (1999), High Maternal Body Weight and Pregnancy Outcome. *Nut Rev* **57**: 62-64

de Onis M, Villar J, Gulmezoglu M, (1998), Nutritional interventions to prevent intrauterine growth retardations: evidence from randomized controlled trials. *Eur J Clin Nutr* **52**: S83-93

Department of Health, (1991), *Dietary Reference Values for Food and Energy and Nutrients for the United Kingdom*. Report on Health and Social Subjects 41. London: TSO.

Department of Health, (1992), *Folic Acid and the prevention of neural tube defects*. Report of an Expert Advisory Committee. London: Department of Health.

Department of Health, (1994), *Weaning and the weaning diet*. Report on Health and Social Subjects 45. London: HMSO.

Department of Health, (1995), *Sensible drinking*. London: HMSO.

Department of Health, (1996), *Guidelines on nutritional assessment of infant formula*. Report on Health and Social Subjects 47. London: HMSO.

Department of Health, (1996), *Low Income, Food, Nutrition and Health: Strategies for improvement.* London: Department of Health

Department of Health, (1998a), Internal Minute.

Department of Health, (1998b), *Nutrition and Bone Health*. Report on Health and Social Subjects 49. London: TSO.

Department of Health, (2000), *Folic Acid and the prevention of Disease*. Report on Health and Social Subjects. London: TSO.

Department of Social Security, (1999a), *Jobseekers Allowance Statistical Enquiry. February 1999*. London: Department of Social Security.

Department of Social Security, (1999b), *Income Support Statistics Quarterly Enquiry. February 1999*. London: Department of Social Security.

Department of Social Security, (1999c), *Family Credit 5% sample of awards. February 1999*. London: Department of Social Security.

Dewey KG, (1998), Growth patterns of breastfed infants and the current status of growth charts for infants. *J Hum Lact* **14**: 89-92

DfEE, (1999a), *Children's Day Care Facilities. Statistical Volume*. London: Department for Education and Employment.

DfEE, (1999b), *Pupils under five years of age in maintained schools in England – January 1998*. SFR 8/1999

DHSS, (1974), *Present Day Practice in Infant feeding*. Report on Health and Social Subjects 9. London: HMSO.

DHSS, (1980), *Present Day Infant Feeding Practice*, Report on Health and Social Subjects 20. London: HMSO.

DHSS, (1988), *Present day practice in infant feeding: third report*. Report on Health and Social Subjects 32. London: HMSO.

Dodds R, (1999), Into the mouths of babes: the government subsidy of infant formula. *The Practising Midwife* **2**: 4-5

Dowdney L, Skuse D, Heptinstall E, Puckering C, Zur-Szpiro S, (1987), Growth retardation and development delay amongst inner city children. *J Child Psychol Psychiat* **28**: 529-541

Dowler E & Calvert C, (1995), *Nutrition and diet in lone-parent families in London*. London: Family and Parenthood, Policy and Practice.

Dowler E, (1998), Food as a utility: ensuring food security for all. *Consumer Policy Review* **8**.

Doyle W, Wynn A, Crawford M, Wynn S, (1992), Nutritional counselling and supplements in the second and third trimester of pregnancy, a study in a London population. *J Nutr Med* **3**: 249-256

Doyle W, (1995), Folic acid in prevention of neural tube defects. *Lancet* **345**: 389-390

Drewett R, Corbett S, Wright C, (1999), Cognitive and educational attainments at school age of children who failed to thrive in infancy: a population based study. *J Child Psychol Psychiat* **40**: 551-561

D'Souza S, Lakham P, Waters H, Bowman K, Cinkotai K, (1987), Iron deficiency in ethnic minorities associations with dietary fibre and phylate. *Early Human Dev* **15**: 103-111

Duggan M, (1993), Cause and cure for iron deficiency in toddlers. *Health Visitor* **66**: 24-26

Duggleby A, Jackson A, (1999), Whole body protein turnover during pregnancy, maternal body composition and fetal outcome. *Proc Nutr Soc* (in press).

Duran-Tauleria E, Rona R, Chinn S, (1995), Factors associated with weight for height and skinfold thickness in British children. *J Epid Comm Health* **49**: 466-473

Eachus J, Williams M, Chan P, Davey-Smith G, Grainge M, Donovan J, Frankel S, (1996), Deprivation and cause specific morbidity: evidence from the Somerset and Avon survey of health. *BMJ* **312**: 287-292

Eaton PM, Wharton PA, Wharton BA, (1984), Nutrient intake of pregnant Asian women at Sorrento Maternity Hospital, Birmingham. *Br J Nutr* **52**: 457-468

Edwards A, Halse P, Parkin J, Waterston A, (1990), Recognising failure to thrive in early childhood. *Arch Dis Child* **65**: 1263-1265

Edwards L, Hellerstadt W, Alton I, Strong M, Himes J, (1996), Pregnancy complications and birth outcomes in obese and normal weight: effects of gestational weight change. *Obstet Gynecol* **87**: 389-394

Ehrhardt P, (1986), Iron deficiency in young Bradford children from different ethnic groups. *BMJ* **292**: 90-93

Ellwood RP & O'Mullane DM, (1996), Identification of areas with high levels of untreated dental caries. *Comm Dent Oral Epidemiol* **24**: 1-6

Elwood PC, Haley TJL, Hughes SJ, Sweetnam PM, Gray OP, Davies DP, (1981), Child growth (0-5-years), and the effect of entitlement to a milk supplement. *Arch Dis Child* **56**:831-835

Emmett P, North K, Noble S, (2000), Types of drinks consumed by young infants. 1. A descriptive study. *Public Health Nutr* **3**: 211-217.

Emond A, Hawkins N, Pennock C, Golding & the ALSPAC Children in Focus Team, (1996), Haemoglobin and ferritin concentrations in infants at 8 months of age. *Arch Dis Child* **74**: 36-39

Fairbank L, Renfrew MJ, Woolridge M, Sowden A, O'Meara S, (2000), A systematic review to evaluate the effectiveness of interventions to promote the uptake of breastfeeding. Health Technology Assessments HTA Programme Monograph 4 (25).

Fairweather-Tait S, (1992), Iron deficiency in infancy: easy to prevent – or is it? *Eur J Clin Nutr* **46**: 9-14

Fall CHD, Yajnik CS, Rao S, Coyaji KJ, Shier RP, (1999), The effects of maternal body composition before pregnancy on fetal growth: The Pnne Maternal and Fetal Growth Study. In *Fetal Programming:* Influences on Development of Disease in Later Life. London: RCOG Press.

FAO, (1988), *Requirements of vitamin A, Iron, Folate and vitamin B12* Report of a joint FAO/WHO Expert Consultation. Rome: Food and Agriculture Organisation.

Farquharson J, Cockburn F, Patrick W, Jamieson E, Logan R, (1992), Infant cerebral cortex phospholipid fatty acid composition and diet. *Lancet* **340**: 810-813

Ferguson A, Mac Donald D, Brydon W (1984), Prevalence of lactase deficiency in British Adults. *Gut* **25**: 163-167

Fleissig A, (1991), Unintended pregnancies and the use of contraception: changes from 1984 to 1989. *BMJ* **302**: 147

Florey C, Leech A, Blackhall A, (1995), Infant feeding and mental and motor development at 18 months of age in first born singletons. *Int J Epidemiol* **1**: 221-222

Forsen T, Erikson JG, Tuomilehto J, Teramok, Osmond C, Barker DJP, (1997), Mother's weight in pregnancy and coronary heart disease in a cogort of Finnish men: follow up study. *BMJ* **35**: 837-840

Foster K, Lader D, Cheesbrough S, (1997), *Infant Feeding 1995*. London: Office for National Statistics.

Freeman JV, Cole TJ, Chinn S, Jones PRM, White E, Preece MA, (1995), Cross-sectional stature and weight reference curves for the UK, 1990. *Arch Dis Child* **73**: 17-24

Gibson S & Williams S, (1999), Dental caries in pre-school children: associations with social class, tooth brushing habit and consumption of sugars and sugar containing foods. Further analysis of data from the National Diet and Nutrition Survey of children aged 1½-4½ years. *Caries Res* **33**: 101-113

Gill DG, Vincent S, Segal DS, (1997), Follow-on formula in the prevention of iron deficiency: a multicentre study. *Acta Paediatrica* **86**: 683-689

Godfrey K, Barker D, Robinson S, Osmond C, (1997), Maternal birthweight and diet in pregnancy in relation to the infant's thinness at birth. *Br J Obstet Gynaecol* **104**: 663-667

Godfrey K, Redman C, Barker D, Osmond C, (1991), The effect of maternal anaemia and iron deficiency on the ratio of fetal weight to placental weight. *Br J Obstet Gynaecol* **98**: 886-891

Godfrey K, Robinson S, Barker DJP, Osmond C, Cox V, (1996), Maternal Nutrition in early and late pregnancy in relation to placental and fetal growth. *BMJ* **312**: 410-414

Godfrey KM, Bernhard BH, Cooper C, (1999), Constraint of the materno-placental supply of nutrients: causes and consequences. In *Fetal Programming: Influences and Development and Disease in Later Life*. eds. O'Brien PM, Wheeler T, Barker DJP. London: RCOG Press.

Goldberg G & Prentice A, (1994), Maternal and Fetal Determinants of Adult Diseases. *Nutr Rev* **52**: 191-200

Golding J, Emmett P, Rogers I, (1997a), Gastro-enteritis, diarrhoea and breastfeeding. *Early Human Development* **49**: S83-S103

Golding J, Emmett P, Rogers I, (1997b), Does breastfeeding protect against non-gastric infections? *Early Human Development* **49**: S105-120

Golding J, Emmett P, Rogers I, (1997c), Does breastfeeding have any impact on non-infectious, non-allergic disorders? *Early Human Development* **49**: S131-142

Golding J, Emmett P, Rogers I, (1997d), Association between breastfeeding, child development and behaviour. *Early Human Development* **49**: S175-84

Gortmaker S, Must A, Perin J, Sobol A, Dietz W, (1993), Social and economic consequences of overweight in adolescence and young adulthood. *New Engl J Med* **329**: 1008-1012

Govan Healthy Eating Project, 1996, *Milk initiative report*. Glasgow: Govan Healthy Eating Project.

Gregory J, Foster K, Tyler H, Wiseman M, (1990), *The Dietary and Nutritional Survey of British Adults*. London: HMSO.

Gregory J, Collins D, Davies P, Hughes J, Clarke P, (1995), *National Diet and Nutrition Survey: children aged 1½-4½ years Volume 1: Report of the Diet and Nutrition Survey*. London: HMSO.

Gregory J & Lowe S, (2000), *National Diet and Nutrition Survey: Young People aged 4-18 years. Volume 1 Report of the Diet and Nutrition Survey*. London : TSO.

Green H & Grishan F,(1983), Excessive fluid intake as a cause of chronic diarrhoea in young children. *J Pediatr* **102**: 836-840

Grindulis H, Scott P, Belton N, Wharton B, (1986), Combined deficiency of iron and vitamin D in Asian toddlers. *Arch Dis Child* **61**: 843-848

Hall D, (1991), *Health for all children*. Second edition. Oxford: Oxford Medical Publications.

Hall D, (1996), *Health for all children*. Third edition Oxford: Oxford University Press.

Hall J, (1995), Midwives and the welfare food scheme. *MIDIRS Midwifery Digest* **5**: 2

Haste F, Brooke O, Anderson H, Bland J, (1991), The effect of nutritional intake on outcome of pregnancy in smokers and non-smokers. *Br J Nutr* **65**: 347-354

Haste F, Brooke O, Anderson H, Bland JM, Shaw A, Griffin J, Peacock J, (1990), Nutrient intakes during pregnancy: observations on the influence of smoking and social class. *Am J Clin Nutr* **51**: 29-36

Health Education Authority, (1999), *Cooking skills*. London: Health Education Authority.

Heinig J & Dewey K, (1997), Health effects of breastfeeding for mothers: a critical review. *Nutr Res Rev* **10**: 35-56

Hendrichse W, Reilly J, Weaver L, (1997), Malnutrition in a children's hospital. *Clin Nutr* **16**: 13-18

Henson S, (1992), From High Street to Hypermarket - food retailing in the 1990s in *Your Food: Whose choice?* ed National Consumer Council. London: HMSO.

HIE, (1999), Rural Scotland Price Survey. www.hie.co.uk

Hinds K & Gregory JR, (1995), *National Diet and Nutrition Survey: children aged 1½-4½ years volume 2: report of the dental survey*. London: HMSO.

Hoddinott P & Pill R, (1999), Qualitative study of decisions about infant feeding among women in east end of London. *BMJ* **318**: 30-34

Holt RD, (1991), Foods and drinks at four daily time intervals in a group of young children. *BDJ* **170**: 137-143

Home Office, (1999), *Asylum Seekers Support. Immigration and Nationality Directorate. March 1999*. London: Home Office.

Høst A, Koletzko B, Dreborg S, Muraro A, Wahn U, Aggett P, Bresson JL, Hernall O, Lafeber H, Michaelson K, Micheli JL, Rigo J, Weaver L, Heymans H, Strobel S, Vandenplas H, (1999), Dietary products used in infants for treatment and prevention of allergy. *Arch Dis Child* **81**: 80-84

Hourihane S & Rolles C, (1995), Morbidity from excessive intake of high energy fluids: the "squash drinking syndrome". *Arch Dis Child* **72**: 141-143

Howie P, Forsyth JS, Ogston A, Clark A, Florey C, (1990), Protective effect of breastfeeding against infection. *BMJ* **300**: 11-16

Hughes J, Li L, Chinn S, Rona R, (1997), Trends in growth in England and Scotland, 1972 to 1994. *Arch Dis Child* **76**: 182-89

Hurrell R, Juillerat M, Reddy M, Lynch S, Dassenko S, Cook J, (1992), Soy protein, phytate and iron absorption in humans. *Am J Clin Nutr* **33**: 746-753

Idjradinata P & Pollitt E, (1993), Reversal of developmental delays in iron deficient anaemic infants treated with iron. *Lancet* **341**: 1-4

Idjradinata P, Watkins W, Pollitt E, (1994), Adverse effect of iron supplementation on weight gain of iron-replete young children. *Lancet* **343**:1252-1254

ISD, (1998), *Small babies in Scotland: a ten year overview: 1987-96*. Edinburgh: ISD Scotland.

Infant formula and follow-on formula regulations, 1995, No 77 Statutory Instruments.

IOM, (1996), *WIC Nutrition Criteria: a scientific assessment*. Washington DC: National Academy Press.

James J, Laing G, Logan S, (1995), Changing patterns of iron deficiency anaemia in the second year of life. *BMJ* **311**: 230

James J, Laing G, Logan S, Rossdale M, (1997), Feasibility of screening toddlers for iron deficiency anaemia in general practice. *BMJ* **315**: 102-103

James, J, Oakhill A, Evans J, (1989a), Preventing iron deficiency in at risk communities. *Lancet* **1**: 40

James J, Lawson P, Male P, Oakhill A, (1989b), Preventing iron deficiency in pre-school children by implementing an educational and screening programme in an inner city practice. *BMJ* **299**: 838-841

Jones S & Hussey R, (1996), Dental health related behaviours in toddlers in low and high caries areas in St Helens, North West England. *BDJ* **181**: 13-17

Jones CM & Worthington H, (1999), The relationship between water fluoridation and socio-economic deprivation on tooth decay in 5-year old children. *BDJ* **186**: 397-400

Kalkwarf, Speker B, Bianchi D, Ran J, Hu M, (1997), The effect of calcium supplementation on bone density during lactation and after weaning. *New Engl J Med* **337**: 523-528

Karlberg J, Jalil F, Lam B, Low L, Yeung C, (1994), Linear growth retardation in relation to the three phases of growth. *Eur J Clin Nutr* **48 (supp 1)**: S25-S44

Kemm J, Douglas J, Sylvester V, (1986), A survey of infant feeding practice by Afro-Carribean mothers in Birmingham. *Hum Nutr: Appl Nutr* **45**: 87A

Kennedy L & Ling M, (1997), Nutrition Education for women in low income groups – is there a role? in *Poverty and Food in Welfare Societies* eds Köhler B, Feichtinger E, Barlösius E and Dowler E, Berlin: Edition Sigma.

Kikuchi S, Rona R, Chinn S, (1995), Physical fitness of 9-year olds in England: related factors. *J Epid Comm Health* **49**: 180-185

Kirk T, (1980), Appraisal of the effectiveness of nutrition education in the context of infant feeding. *J Hum Nutr* **34**: 429-438

Landon J & Thorpe L, (1998), *Changing preconceptions: The HEA Folic Acid campaign 1995-8: volume 1*. London:Health Education Authority.

Land A, Lowe R, Whiteside N, (1992), *The Development of the Welfare State 1939-1951*. London: HMSO.

Lansdown R & Wharton B, (1995), Iron and mental and motor behaviour in children. in *Iron: nutritional and physiological significance*. British Nutrition Foundation. London: Chapman and Hall.

Lawson MS, Thomas M, Hardiman A, (1998), Iron status of Asian children aged 2 years living in England. *Arch Dis Child* **78**: 420-426

Lawson M & Thomas M, (1999a), Vitamins D concentrations in Asian children aged 2 years living in England: population survey. *BMJ* **318**: 28

Lawson M, Thomas M, Hardiman A, (1999b), Dietary factors affecting plasma vitamin D levels in Asian children living in England. *Eur J Clin Nutr* **53**: 268-272

Leather S, (1992), Less Money, Less Choice: poverty and diet in the UK today in *Your Food: Whose choice?* ed National Consumer Council. London: HMSO.

Leather, S, (1996), Modern Malnutrition: an overview of poverty in the UK. Caroline Walker Trust Lecture 1996. London: Caroline Walker Trust.

Lifshitz F & Ament M, (1992), Role of juice carbohydrate malabsorption in chronic non-specific diarrhoea in children. *J Pediatr* **120**: 825-829

Logan S, (1999), Commentary: iron deficiency anaemia and developmental deficit – the jury is still out. *BMJ* **318**: 697-698

MAFF, (1994), *The Dietary and Nutritional Survey of British Adults – Further Analysis*. London: HMSO.

MAFF, (1996), *Statement by the COT on phytoestrogens*. Food Surveillance paper no 57: 58-81. London: Ministry of Agriculture, Fisheries and Food.

MAFF, (1998), *National Food Survey 1997*. London: TSO.

Makrides M, Neumann M, Byard R, Simmer K, Gibson R, (1994), Fatty acid composition of brain, retina and erythrocytes in breast- and formula fed infants *Am J Clin Nutr* **60**: 189-194

Maternity Alliance, (1995), *Poor expectations: poverty and undernutrition in poverty*. London: National Children's Home.

Mathews F, (1996), Antioxidant nutrients in pregnancy: a systematic review of the literature. *Nutr Res Rev* **9**: 175-195

Mathews F, Yudkin P, Neil A, (1998), Folates in the periconceptional period: are women getting enough? *Br J Obstet Gynaecol* **105**: 954-959

Mathews F & Neil H, (1998), Nutrient intakes during pregnancy in a cohort of nulliparous women. *J Hum Nutr Diet* **11**:151-161

Mathews F, Yudkin P, Neil A, (1999), Influence of maternal nutrition on outcome in pregnancy: prospective cohort study. *BMJ* **319**: 339-343

Mathews F, Yudkin P, Smith R, Neil A, (2000), Nutrient intakes during pregnancy: the influence of smoking status and age. *J Epid Comm Health* **54**: 17-23

McInnes R & Tappin D, (1996), Value of milk tokens for breastfeeding mothers should be increased. *BMJ* **313**: 1484-1485

McInnes R, (1998), *An evaluation of a community based intervention designed to increase the prevalence of breastfeeding in a socially disadvantaged urban area.* PEACH Paper No 7. Glasgow: University of Glasgow.

McIntosh J, (1985), Barriers to breastfeeding: choice of feeding method in a sample of working class primiparae. *Midwifery* **1**: 213-224

McIntosh J, (1986), Weaning practices in a sample of working class primiparae. *Child: care health and development* **12**: 215-226

Mehta K, Specker B, Bartholmey S, Giddens J, Ho M, (1998), Trial on timing of introduction to solids and food type on infant growth. *Pediatrics* **102**:569-573

Meimendinger J, Laird N, Austin J, Timmer P, Gershoff S, (1984), The effects of the WIC program on the growth of infants. *Am J Clin Nutr* **40**: 1250-1257

Meis P, Michielutte R, Peters T, Bradley Wells H, Evan Sands R, Coles E, Johns K, (1997), Factors associated with term low birth weight in Cardiff, Wales. *Paediatric & Perinatal Epidemiology* **11**: 287-297

Mills A, (1990), Surveillance for anaemia: risk factors in patterns of milk intake. *Arch Dis Child* **65**: 428-431

Mills A & Tyler H, (1992), *Food and Nutrient Intakes of British Infants aged 6-12 months*. London: Ministry of Agriculture, Fisheries and Food.

Ministry of Health, (1957), *Report of the Joint Sub-Committee on Welfare Foods*. London: HMSO.

Moffat M, Longstaffe S, Besant J, Dureski C, (1994), Prevention of iron deficiency and psychomotor decline in high-risk infants through use of iron-fortified infant formula: a randomised clinical trial. *J Pediatrics* **125**: 5277-5284

Morley R, Abbott R, Fairweather-Tait, MacFadyen U, Stephenson T, Lucas A, (1999), Iron fortified follow on formula from 9 to 18 months improves iron status but not development or growth: a randomised trial. *Arch Dis Child* **81**: 247-252

Mughal M, Salama H, Greenaway T, Laing I, Mawer, (1999), Florid rickets associated with prolonged breastfeeding without vitamin D supplementation. *BMJ* **318**: 39-40

Mulligan J, Voss LD, McCaughey ES, Bailey BJ, Betts PR, (1998), Growth monitoring: testing the new guidelines, *Arch Dis Child* **79**: 318-322

Murphy J, O'Riordan J, Newcombe R, Coles E, Pearson J, (1986), Relation of Haemoglobin levels in first and second trimesters to outcome of pregnancy. *Lancet* **1**: 992-994

National Breastfeeding Working Group, (1995), *Breastfeeding good practice guidance to the NHS*. London: Department of Health.

Nazroo J, (1997), *The Health of Britain's Ethnic Minorities*. London: PSI.

Nazroo JY, (1998), Genetic, cultural or socio-economic vulnerability? Explaining ethnic inequalities in health. *Sociology of Health and Illness* **20**: 710-730

NCH, (1991), *NCH Poverty and Nutrition Survey* (1991). London: National Children's Home.

NCT, (1999), *The Access Project*. National Childbirth Trust. Preliminary data.

Nelson M & Paul A, (1983), The nutritive contribution of school dinners and other mid day meals to the diets of school children. *Hum Nutr: Appl Nutr* **37A**: 128-135

NHS Executive, (1995), Health Service Guidelines: welfare food scheme updated guidance. HSG (95) 30

NHS Executive, (1996), Health Service Guidelines: welfare food scheme updated guidance. HSG (96) 44

North K, Emmett P, Noble S, (2000), Types of drinks consumed by young infants: II Socio-demographic variations. Submitted to *J Human Nutriti Dietet* **13**:71-82

Oddy W, Holt P, Sly P, Read A, Landau L, Stanley F, Kendall G, Burton P, (1999), Association between breastfeeding and asthma in 6 year old children: findings of a prospective birth cohort study. *BMJ* **319**: 815-819

Ong S, Ryley J, Bashir T, MacDonald, (1983), Nutrient intake and associated biochemical status of pregnant Asians in the United Kingdom. *Hum Nutr: Appl Nutr* **37 A**: 23-29

Office of National Statistics, (1998a), *Family spending: a report of the 1997-98 Family Expenditure Survey.* London: TSO.

Office of National Statistics, (1998b), *Social Trends 28.* London: TSO.

Office of National Statistics, (1999a), *Mortality Statistics: childhood, infant and perinatal, 1997 series DH3 no30* London: TSO.

Office of National Statistics, (1999b), *Annual Abstracts of Statistics.* London: TSO.

Office of National Statistics, (1999c), *Social Trends 29.* London: TSO.

Owens B, (1997), *Out of the frying pan: the true cost of feeding a family on low income.* London: Save the Children Fund.

Owen A & Owen G, (1997), Twenty years of WIC: a review of some effects of the program. *J Am Diet Assoc* **97**: 777-782

Parker H, (1998), *Low cost but acceptable, a minimum income standard for the UK.* London: Family Budget Unit.

Parsons T, Power C, Logan S, Summerbell, (1999), *Childhood Predictors of Adult Obesity*: a systematic review. Int J Obes Relat Metab Disord 23 supp 8:51-107

Payne J & Belton N, (1992), Nutrient intake and growth in pre-school children. II Intake of minerals and vitamins. *J Hum Nutr Diet* **5**: 299-304

Perry I, Beevers D, Whincup P, Bareford D, (1995), Predictors of ratio of placental weight to fetal weight in multiethnic community. *BMJ* **310**: 436-439

Piachaud D & Webb W, (1996), *The price of food – missing out on mass consumption*. Suntory and Toyota International Centres of Economics and related Disciplines. London: London School of Economics.

Policy Action Team 13, (1999), Bringing Britain Together: national strategy for neighbourhood renewal, report of policy action team 13: improving shopping access.

Poppendieck J, (1997), The USA: Hunger in the Land of Plenty in *First World Hunger* ed. Riches G. Cambridge: Cambridge University Press.

Power C, Lake J, Cole T, (1997a), Measurement and long-term risks of child and adolescent fatness. *Int J Obes Relat Metab Disord* **21**: 507-526

Power C, Lake J, Cole T, (1997b), Body mass index and height from childhood to adulthood in the British 1958 birth cohort. *Am J Clin Nutr* **66**: 1094-1101

Power R, (1999), *Promoting the health of homeless people: setting a research agenda*. London: Health Education Authority.

Prentice A & Prentice A, (1995), Evolutionary and environmental influences on human lactation. *Proc Nutr Soc* **54**: 391-400

Prentice A, Jargon L, Cole T, Stirling D, Dibba B, Fairweather Tait S, (1995), Calcium requirements of lactating Gambian mother: effects of a calcium supplement on breastmilk calcium concentrations, maternal bone mineral content, and urinary calcium excretion. *Am J Clin Nutr* **62**: 58-67

Prentice A & Jebb S, (1995), Obesity in Britain: gluttony or sloth. *BMJ* **311**: 437-439

Prentice A, Spaaij G, Poppitt S, van Raaij S, Totton M, Swann D, Black A, (1996), Energy requirements of pregnant and lactating women *En J Clin Nut* **50: supp 1** 82-111

Prentice A & Goldberg G, (1996), Maternal Obesity Increases Congenital Malformations. *Nutr Rev* **54:** 146-152

Prentice A *et al*, (2000), Maternal calcium metabolism and bone mineral status, *Am J Clin Nutr* **71**: 1312S-1316S

Prescott-Clarke P & Primatesta P, (1998), *Health Survey for England: the health of young people 1995-97 vol 1: findings*. Joint Health Surveys Unit. London: TSO.

Provart S & Carmichael C, (1995), The use of an index of material deprivation to identify groups of children at risk to dental caries in County Durham. *Comm Dent Health* **12**: 138-142

Raiten D, Talbot J, Waters J eds, (1998), Assessment of nutritional requirements for infant formulas. Life Sciences Research Unit.

Raynor P & Rudolf M, (1996), What do we know about children who fail to thrive? *Child: care, health and development* **22**: 241-250

Raynor P, Rudolf M, Cooper K, Marchant P, Cottrell D, (1999), A randomised controlled trial of specialist health visitor interventions for failure to thrive. *Arch Dis Child* **80**: 500-506

Riley J, Lennon M, Ellwood R, (1999), The effect of water fluoridation and social inequalities on dental caries in 5 year old children: *Int J Epid* **28**: 300-305

Robinson S, Godfrey K, Denne J, Cox V, (1998), The determinants of iron status in pregnancy. *Br J Nutr* **79**: 249-255

Robinson S, Godfrey K, Osmond C, Barker D, (1996), Evaluation of a food frequency questionnaire used to assess nutrient intakes in pregnant women. *Eur J Clin Nutr* **50**: 302-308

Rogers I, Emmett P & the ALSPAC Study Team, (1998a), Diet during pregnancy in a population of pregnant women in South West England. *Eur J Clin Nutr* **52**, 246-250

Rogers I, Emmett P, Baker D, Golding J & the ALSPAC Study Team, (1998b), Financial difficulties, smoking habits, composition of the diet and birth weight in a population of pregnant women in the South West of England. *Eur J Clin Nutr* **52**: 251-260

Rogers I, Emmett P, Golding J, (1997), The growth and nutritional status of the breast-fed infant. *Early Human Development* **49**: S157-74

Rolland-Cachera MF, Deheeger M, Akrout M, Bellisle F, (1995), Influence of macronutrients on adiposity development: a follow-up study of nutrition and growth from 10 months to 8-years of age. *Int J Obes Relat Metab Disord* **19**: 573-578

Rona R & Chinn S, (1989), School meals, school milk and height of primary school children in England and Scotland in the eighties. *J Epid Comm Health* **43**: 66-71

Rona R & Chinn S, (1995), Genetic and environmental influences on growth. *J Med Screening* **2**: 133-139

Rona R, Qureshi S, Chinn S, (1996), Factors related to total cholesterol and blood pressure in British 9-year olds. *J Epid Comm Health* **50**: 512-518

Rose D, Habicht J-P, Devaney B, (1997), Household participation in the food stamp and WIC programs increases the nutrient intakes of preschool children. *J Nutr* **128**: 548-555

RSGB, (1989), Usage of and attitudes towards milk among low income families. Research Surveys of Great Britain ref 5421.

Rudat K, (1994), *Black and minority ethnic groups in England, health and lifestyles*. London: Health Education Authority.

Savage S-A, Reilly J, Edwards C, Durnin J, (1998), Weaning practice in the Glasgow longitudinal infant growth study. *Arch Dis Child* **79**: 153-156

Schofield C, Stewart J, Wheeler E, (1989), The diets of pregnant and post pregnant women in different social groups in London and Edinburgh: calcium, iron, retinol, ascorbic acid and folic acid. *Br J Nutr* **62**: 363-377

Serdula M, Ivery D, Coates R, Freedman D, Williams D, Byers T, (1993), Do obese children becomes obese adults? A review of the literature. *Prev Med* **22**: 167-177

Sharma A, Lynch M, Irvine M, (1994), The availability of advice regarding infant feeding to immigrants of Vietnamese origin: a survey of families and health visitors. *Child: care, health and development* **20**: 349-354

Shea S, Stein AD, Basch CE, Contento IR, Zybert P, (1990), Variability and self regulation of energy intake in young children in their every day environment. *Pediatrics* **90**: 542-546

Shelter week, (1998), *Behind closed doors: the real extent of homelessness and housing need*. London: Shelter.

Sherriff A, Emond A, Hawkins N, Golding J & the ALSPAC Children in Focus Study Team, (1999), Haemoglobin and ferritin concentrations in children aged 12 and 18 months. *Arch Dis Child* **80**: 153-157

Skinner J, Carruth B, Moran J, Houck K, Colletta F, (1999), Fruit juice is not related to children's growth. *Pediatrics* **103**: 58-64

Skuse D, Reilly S, Wolke D, (1994), Psychosocial adversity and growth during infancy. *Eur J Clin Nutr* **48**: 113-130

Smith R, Davies N & Davies J, (1994), Prevention of neural tube defects. *Lancet* **343**: 123

Social Exclusion Unit, 1999, *Teenage Pregnancy*. London: TSO.

Stevens D & Nelson A, (1995), The effect of iron in formula milk after 6 months of age. *Arch Dis Child* **73**, 216-220

Stevens D, (1998), Screening toddlers for iron deficiency anaemia in general practice. *BMJ* **316**: 145-146

Summerbell C, Moody RC, Shanks J, Stock MJ, Geissler C, (1996), Relationship between feeding pattern and body mass index in 220 free-living people in four age groups. *Eur J Clin Nutr* **50**: 513-519

Sutcliffe M, Schorah C, Perry A, Wild J, (1993), Prevention of neural-tube defects. *Lancet* **342**:1174

Sutcliffe M, Wild J, Perry A & Schorah C, (1994), Prevention of neural-tube defects. *Lancet* **344**: 1578

Tamhne R, (1998), Study to determine prevalence of iron deficiency was suspended. *BMJ* **316**: 146

Tanner JM, (1989), *Foetus into Man*. London: Castlemead Publications.

Tanner J, (1992), Growth as a measure of the nutritional and hygienic status of a population. *Horm Res* **38**: **Suppl**:106-115

Thomas M & Avery V, (1997), *Infant Feeding in Asian Families*. London: TSO.

Tickle M, Williams M, Jenner T, Blinkhorn A, (1999), The effects of socio-economic status and dental attendance on dental caries experience, and treatment patterns in 5-year-old children. *BDJ* **186**: 135-137

Treem W, (1992), Chronic non specific diarrhoea in childhood. *Clinical Pediatrics* **31**: 413-420

TSO, (1999a), *Congenital Anomalies 1998*. MB3 no 13. London: TSO.

TSO, (1999b), *Abortion Statistics 1998*, Series ARV AB no 25. London: TSO.

TSO, (1999c), *Saving Lives: Our healthier nation*. London: TSO.

UNICEF-UK Baby Friendly Initiative, (1999a), *Towards National Regional and Local Strategies for breastfeeding*. London: UNICEF.

UNICEF-UK Baby Friendly Initiative, (1999b), The Baby Friendly Initiative in the community: a seven point plan for protection, promotion and support of breastfeeding in community health care settings. London: UNICEF.

Victor C, (1997), The health of homeless people in Britain: a review. *Eur J Pub Health* **7**: 398-404

Viegas O, Scott P, Cole T, Mansfield P, Wharton P & Wharton B, (1982a), Dietary protein energy supplementation of pregnant Asian mothers at Sorrento, Birmingham I: Selective during third trimester only. *BMJ* **285**: 592-595

Von Kreis R, Koletzko B, Sauerwald T, von Mutius E, Barnert D, Grunert V, von Voss H, (1999), Breastfeeding and Obesity: cross sectional study. *BMJ* **319**: 147-150

Voss L, (1999),Changing Practice in Growth Monitoring. *BMJ* **318**: 344-345

Voss L, Mulligan J & Betts P, (1998), *Child Care health and development* **24**: 145-156

Warrington S & Storey D, (1989), Iron Deficiency in Young Rochdale Children. *J Roy Soc Health* **109**: 64-65

Welfare Foods Order, (1968), Part II 3 (1) Statutory Instruments No 389

Welfare Food Regulations, (1996), No 1434 Statutory Instrument

Welfare Food Regulations (Northern Ireland), (1988) No.137

Welfare Food Scheme, (1995), Policy Statement. Internal document, Department of Health

Welfare Food Scheme, (1999), draft position paper on disabled children's milk scheme.

Wharfe L, (1999), The welfare foods scheme, a summary report of a survey carried out by Liz Wharfe on behalf of NCVCCO / Department of Health.

Wharton B, (1999), Low plasma vitamin D in Asian toddlers. *BMJ* **318**: 2-3

White E, Wilson A, Greene SA, Berry W, McCowan C, Cairns A, Ricketts I, (1995), Growth screening and urban deprivation *J Med Screening* **2**: 140-144

WHO, (1981), *International Code of Marketing of Breastmilk Substitutes*. Geneva: World Health Organisation.

WHO, (1991), *Indicators for assessing breastfeeding practice*. Report of an informal meeting. 11-12 June 1991. Geneva: World Health Organisation.

WHO, (1998), *Evidence for the ten steps to successful breastfeeding*. Family and Reproductive Health, Division of child health and development. Geneva: World Health Organisation.

WHO, (1998a), *Complementary Feeding of Young People in developing Countries*. Geneva: World Health Organisation.

Wilcox M, Smith S, Johnson I, Maynard P, Chilvers C (1995), The effect of social deprivation on birth weights excluding physiological and pathological effects. *Br J Obs & Gynae* **102**: 918-924

Wild J, Schorah C, Maude K, Levene M, (1996), Folate intake in young women and their knowledge of pre-conceptional folate supplementation to prevent neural tube defects. *Eur J Obs Gynae* **70**: 185-189

Wilkinson RG, (1999), Putting the picture together: prosperity, redistribution, health and welfare, in *Social Determinants of Health* eds Marmot M & Wilkinson RG. Oxford: Oxford University Press.

Williams J, Wolff A, Daly A, MacDonald A, Aukett A, Booth I, (1999), Iron supplemented formula milk related to reduction in psychomotor decline in infants from inner city areas: randomised study. *BMJ* **318**: 693-698

Wilson A, Forsyth J, Greene S, Irvine L, Hau C & Howie P, (1998), Relation of infant diet to childhood health: seven year follow-up of cohort of children in Dundee infant feeding study. *BMJ* **316**: 21-25

Wright C, Callum J, Birks E, Jarvis S, (1998), Effect of Community based management in failure to thrive: randomised controlled trial. *BMJ* **317**: 571-574

Wright C, Loughridge J, Moore J, (2000), Failure to thrive in a population context: two contrasting studies of feeding and nutritional status. *Proc Nutr Soc* **59**: 37-45

Wright C, Matthews J, Waterston A, Aynsley-Green A, (1994a), What is a normal rate of weight gain in infancy? *Acta Paediatr* **83**: 351-356

Wright C, Waterson A, Aynsley-Green A, (1994b), Effect of deprivation on weight gain in infancy. *Acta Paediatr* **83**: 357-359

Wright C & Talbot E, (1996), Screening for failure to thrive – what are we looking for? *Child: care, health and development* **22**: 223-234

Wylie J & Verber I, (1994), Why women fail to breastfeed: a prospective study from booking to 28 days post partum. *J Hum Nutr Diet* **7**: 115-120

Wynn A, Crawford M, Doyle W, Wynn S, (1991), Nutrition of women in anticipation of gnancy. *Nutrition and Health* **7**: 69-88

Wynn SW, Wynn AHA, Doyle W, Crawford MA, (1994), The association of maternal social class with maternal diet and the dimensions of babies in a population of London women. *Nutrition and Health* **9**: 303-315

Yip R, Binkin N, Fleshood L, Trowbridge F, (1987b), Declining prevalence of anaemia among low income children in the United States. *JAMA* **258**: 1619-1623

Yip R, Parvanta I, Scanlon K, Borland E, Russell C, Trowbridge F, (1992), Pediatric nutrition surveillance system – United States 1980-91. *Morb Mortal Wkly Rep CDC Surveill Summ* **41**: 1-24

Yip R, Walsh K, Goldfarb M, Binkin N, (1987a), Declining prevalence of anaemia in childhood in a middle class setting: a pediatric success story? *Pediatrics* **80**: 330-334

Zhou W & Olsen J, (1997), Gestational weight gain as a predictor of birth and placenta weight according to pre-pregnancy body mass index. *Acta Obstet Gynaecol Scand* **76**: 300-307

Zlotkin S, (1999), Vitamin D concentrations in Asian children living in England. *BMJ* **318**: 1417